Penny Haren's
Pieced Appliqué™

Landauer Books

Penny Haren's
Pieced Appliqué™

Copyright© 2009 by Landauer Corporation

Pieced Appliqué™ projects
Copyright© 2008 by Penny Haren

This book was designed, produced, and published by
Landauer Books
A division of Landauer Corporation
3100 101st Street, Urbandale, IA 50322
www.landauercorp.com   800/557-2144

President/Publisher: Jeramy Lanigan Landauer
Vice President of Sales and Operations: Kitty Jacobson
Managing Editor: Jeri Simon
Art Director: Laurel Albright
Photographer: Sue Voegtlin

ISBN 13: 978-0-9800688-4-9
ISBN 10:   0-9800688-4-3

Library of Congress Control Number: 2008933526

This book printed on acid-free paper.
Printed in China

10-9-8-7-6-5-4-3-2-1

Foreword

This is my second book of 6" finished blocks using the Pieced Appliqué™ technique. And, due to the enthusiastic response from all of you, there will be many more blocks to come.

I see quilt blocks in layers—like a three dimensional tic-tac-toe board I had as a child. I did not realize until I opened a quilt shop that most people see blocks as jigsaw puzzles. This fact came to my attention when students were driving several hours to participate in classes. My Pieced Appliqué™ technique came to the attention of some folks on the national level. And, as they say, the rest is history!

As the mother of five, I firmly believe that it takes a village to raise a child. In my case, it took amazing mentors to create an author! And, believe me, I could not have done it without them. Keeping me focused— and my creative juices flowing on one project at a time—is not easy!

Jenny Stratton, Rob Krieger, and Jeramy Landauer have opened so many doors for me and have made all of my dreams come true! I am so blessed to call them friends. They have each enriched my life in more ways than I ever imagined.

And, I honestly don't see what they get out of this relationship— except I do make them laugh on a fairly regular basis! Thank God they have a sense of humor.......

I get my own comic relief from my quilting friends. In this case there are four ladies who heard me whine about deadlines for this book—and came to my rescue. They would show up at my door, bright and early, machines in tow, and sew until the wee hours of the morning. How do you thank friends like that? I appreciate all of their help and thank Charlotte Smith, Helene Bednarczuk, Nada Garvin, and Sherry Ross for the quilts in this book.

Love,
Penny

Table of Contents

Liberty Star

22

Homemaker

28

Cross Roads

34

True Lover's Knot

40

Kansas Dug-Out

42

Weathervane

46

Cornerstone

50

Christmas Star

52

5

Table of Contents

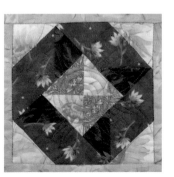

Every finished Pieced Appliqué™ block is built on an easy-to-make foundation block. The name of the foundation block you need to make for each finished block is given at the beginning of the instructions.

Everything you need to know to successfully create beautiful archival blocks you may have thought impossible is here.

Introducing Foundation Blocks

Begin with Basic *Finish with Beautiful*

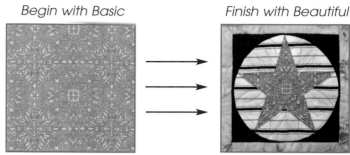

6-1/2" Foundation Block

Four-Patch
Foundation Block

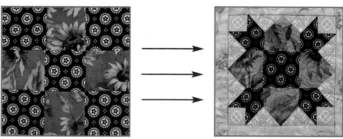

Nine-Patch
Foundation Block

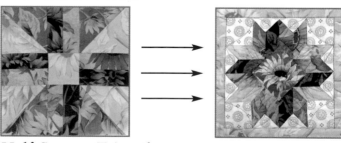

Half-Square Triangles
Foundation Block

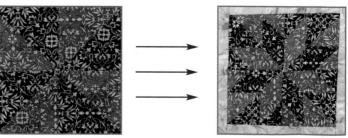

Pinwheel Foundation Block

8

Kaleidoscope
Foundation Block

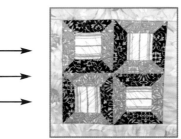

Quarter-Square Triangles
Foundation Block

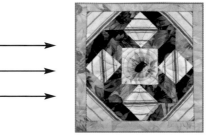

Set on Point
Foundation Block

Bright Hopes
Foundation Block

Pennsylvania
Foundation Block

To create the Pieced Appliqué™ blocks on the following pages, you will need approximately 18 fat quarters—6 each of neutral, medium, and dark. This is only an estimation. Fussy cutting will affect the yardage needed. You may also use an assortment of scraps, fat eighths, and fat quarters if you prefer more variety in your finished quilt. Turn the page to begin. Enjoy!

General Instructions

Introducing Pieced Appliqué™

Pieced Appliqué™ is an innovative new technique to create traditional pieced blocks with more accuracy and ease than the current methods. Even a beginner can create complicated blocks—even miniature blocks—with excellent results.

With Pieced Appliqué™

- You see exactly what your finished block will look like before anything is stitched.
- You position and appliqué points and curves for perfect placement without machine piecing.
- You create blocks with very sharp points and curves that are impossible to achieve with traditional methods.
- You eliminate puckers created by piecing inset points and "Y" seams by appliquéing them.
- You can carry your blocks with you to work on wherever you go.

Creating Pieced Appliqué™ Blocks in 5 Easy Steps

1 **Create an easy foundation block**

2 **Make paper templates and iron on freezer paper**

3 **Glue the template to the wrong side of the fabric and turn with a glue stick**

4 **Stitch the appliqués to the foundation block to create the desired archival block**

5 **Remove the paper templates by soaking the block in warm water to dissolve the glue, then dry and press the completed block**

The Pieced Appliqué™ Process

Making the Foundation Blocks:
The first step in the Pieced Appliqué™ process is making your foundation block.

Making the Paper Templates:
To make the paper templates for your appliqués, either photocopy the template patterns shown with the block instructions or trace the template patterns onto white typing paper.

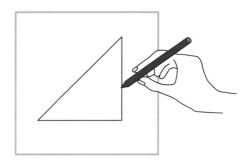

• Adding the Freezer Paper:
Place the photocopied paper pattern face down on the ironing board so that any water in the iron does not smear the ink on the copy. Place the waxy side of the freezer paper on top of the **BLANK** side of the copied paper templates. Freezer paper is available at grocery stores in the paper products aisle or in 8-1/2" x 11" sheets at your local quilt shop.

Note: *To download a complete set of templates for all the blocks in this book, in the multiples needed, visit www.landauercorp.com. Some printers will shrink these templates to fit preset margins. Run one copy and check it against the templates in the book to be sure they are printing at 100%.*

TIP

Some copiers distort images more than others. Check your copies for accuracy by comparing your templates to the templates in the book. If your copier distorts the pattern too much, you will have to trace the pattern onto white typing paper or find another copier. My own copier tends to distort in one direction about 1/16". I can live with that.

Make sure that the ink from your copies will not bleed and discolor the fabric when wet. We have not had any problems with this yet, but there is always that chance. Better safe than sorry.

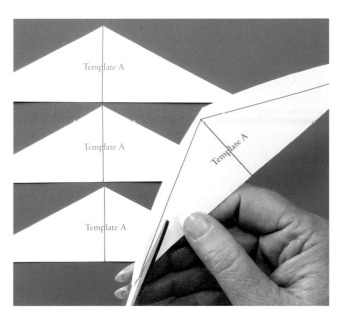

Template A

Template A

Template A

Template A

• Cutting Out the Paper Templates:
When cutting out the paper templates, be sure to cut just **INSIDE** photocopied (or drawn) lines to allow for the thickness of the fabric when turning the fabric over the template to make the appliqué.

General Instructions

Preparing and Cutting the Fabric Appliqué

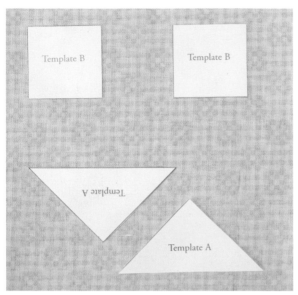

Glue the **BLANK** side of the freezer paper template onto the wrong side of the fabric. The printing on the freezer paper template should be face up.

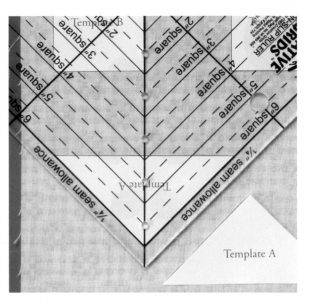

Place the ruler on the template and measure to provide for a 1/4" seam allowance. Use a rotary cutter to trim the fabric exactly 1/4" away from the paper template on all sides. If you are using the Creative Grids™ *Square It Up & Fussy Cut* ruler, the 1/4" seam is marked for you.

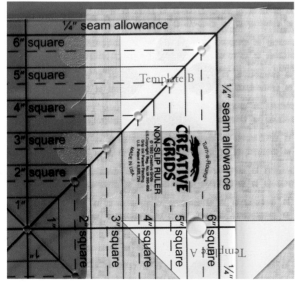

By placing the corner of the ruler on the template, you can trim two sides at once.

TIP

When you are told to trim the fabric exactly 1/4" away from the template, it is not a suggestion. By trimming 1/4" away, you are adding an accurate seam allowance to the appliqué which will help you position the appliqué on your foundation block. Since all curved sides are turned, you can estimate the 1/4" seam allowance on those edges.

Turning the Appliqués
Turning Straight Edges and Corners:

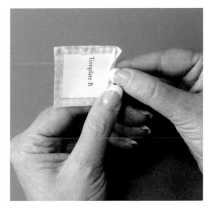

Run a glue stick along the edge of the paper template and the edge of the fabric to be turned. Be sure to run the glue past the template into the seam allowance.

Turn the edge of the wrong side of the fabric over the template using your thumbnail and move forward 1/8" at a time. At the corner turn the fabric so it is angled slightly down.

When the right angle is turned, the seam allowance for the second side will be totally hidden by the template.

Note: In block instructions the sides of the templates to be turned are marked with an ∗. Unturned sides are the seam allowances.

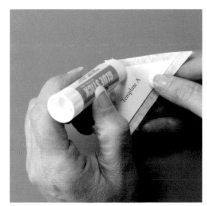

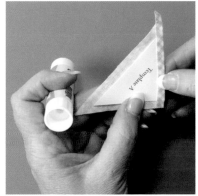

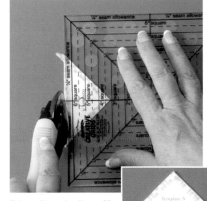

When turning a triangle, glue and turn the two sides just like a square.

This will create "tails" on the bottom raw edge of the triangle.

Trim the tails off even with the seam allowance.

TIP

I use white paste glue sticks to turn my appliqués. Don't purchase the purple, pink, and blue ones. You don't want to risk dyes coming back at a later date. Buy the large packages of glue sticks and keep them in the refrigerator. The moist environment stops them from drying out and they will last up to a year. When you are not using your glue stick, put the lid back on. They dry out very quickly if you leave the top off while turning each piece.

Turning the Appliqués

Turning Outside Curves:

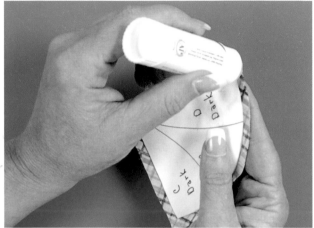

Some blocks have appliqués with curves. When turning an outside curve trim the fabric approximately 1/4" away from the curved side of the template. Turn and gather the fabric around the template. Do not clip outside curves. If you have rough edges on your appliqué, turn it over to the wrong side. You will notice there are pleats on the folded edge of your piece. While the glue is still wet, place a fingernail on each side of the "pleat" and pull it down to the correct shape. The straight edges should be trimmed exactly 1/4" away from the template.

Turning Inside Curves:

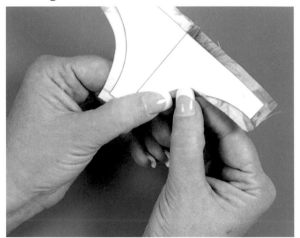

To turn an inside curve, trim the fabric approximately 1/4" away from the curved sides of the template. The inside curve of this appliqué does not have to be clipped. Since it is a gentle curve and the straight side of the template is placed on the grain line of the fabric, the curve is automatically placed on the bias and turns easily with no clipping required. The straight edges should be trimmed exactly 1/4" away from the template.

Turning Inner Circles:

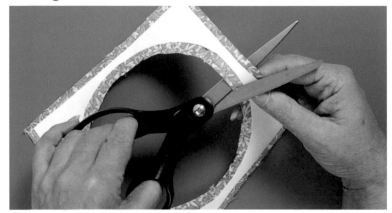

In the picture above, the center circle must be cut out approximately 1/4" away from the inner circle of the template. The seam allowance must be clipped in order to turn the fabric over the template. The straight edges should be trimmed exactly 1/4" away from the template.

Run a glue stick along the edge of the paper template and fabric. Turn the edge of the wrong side of the fabric over the template. Move your thumbnail forward 1/8" at a time.

Layering One Appliqué Over Another

Hand Appliqué

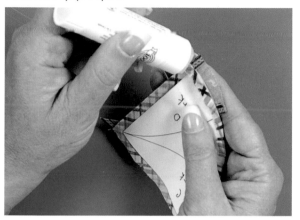

Some blocks require one appliqué to be placed on top of another. If you are going to hand appliqué, glue the wrong side of the top appliqué to the right side of the bottom appliqué.

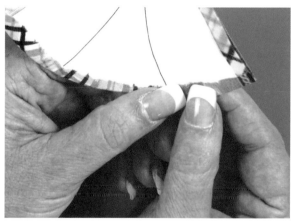

The raw edge of the top appliqué is then glued and turned over the edge of the bottom appliqué. When you hand appliqué, you will catch the fabric edges of both appliqués with your needle and thread while avoiding the paper template.

Machine Appliqué

If you are going to machine appliqué, the appliqués must be glued to the foundation block and sewn, one layer at a time, so the templates can be removed before the next layer of appliqués is stitched in place. You do not want to sew the templates into your finished block. Continue to machine appliqué and remove the templates, one layer at a time, until the block is complete.

Turn all pieces before appliquéing any in place to ensure that subsequent layers of appliqués will cover and match the layer below it.

TIP

Clip inside points and curves to within a few threads of the template to aid in turning. Do not clip outside curves. Every cut is a potential weakness in your project.

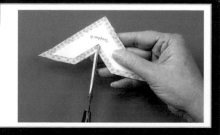

Cutting Appliqués from a Pieced Block

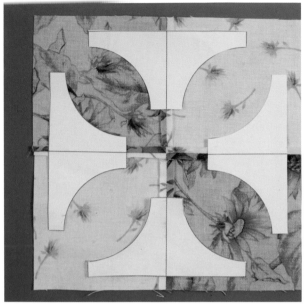

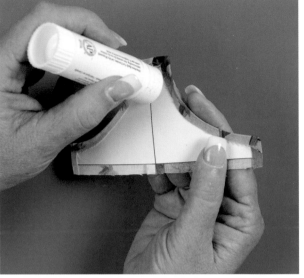

Some of the Pieced Appliqué™ blocks require two foundation blocks. One of the blocks will be used to cut the appliqués, as demonstrated in the photo above. Place the lines of the paper template on the seam lines of the wrong side of the pieced block and trim 1/4" away from the templates on all sides.

Glue and turn the sides of the appliqué as instructed in the block directions. In the picture above, the inside curve of the appliqué does not have to be clipped. Since it is a gentle curve and the straight side of the template is placed on the grain line of the fabric, the curve is automatically placed on the bias and turns easily.

Run glue on the wrong side of the template. Match the seam lines of the appliqué to the seam lines of the foundation block and glue in place. Do not place glue on the seam allowance. You don't want to stitch through it later.

Rotate the block as you place the appliqués. Since the appliqués were trimmed exactly 1/4" away from the templates, place the raw edges even with the raw edges of the foundation block.

Stitching the Appliqué Templates
Thread

Use only high quality cotton thread or cotton wrapped polyester. Not all threads are created equal.

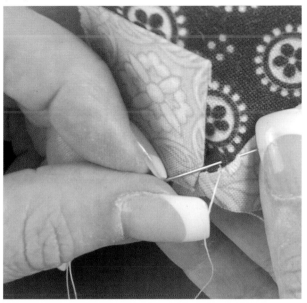

Hand stitch the turned edges of the appliqué, using an invisible appliqué stitch. Leave the raw edges open. If your appliquéd pieces are layered, only stitch to the fabric directly below. Do not go clear down to the foundation block. You don't want to sew the paper templates into your work. Take a few extra stitches to reinforce any areas that were clipped because of inside curves. Knots should be hidden beneath the appliqué piece. Do not place your knot on the wrong side of the foundation square. The thread tail could shadow through the finished block.

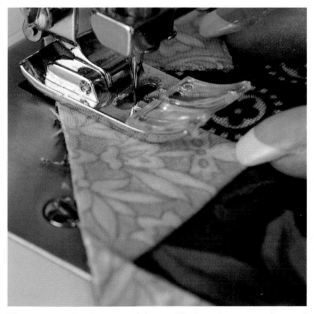

If you prefer to machine stitch, use a narrow zigzag stitch with invisible thread in the top of your machine and 50 or 60 weight thread in the bobbin. If your appliqué pieces are layered, stitch the bottom appliqué first. Remove the paper templates and press your block. Glue the second layer of appliqués to your block and stitch them in place. Remove the paper templates and glue, following directions on pages 18-19.

Removing the Paper Templates and Glue

When the stitching is done, place the appliquéd block into warm water for at least twenty minutes. This will dissolve the glue.

Remove the appliquéd block from the water and squeeze out the excess water.

Roll the block in an absorbent towel to remove any remaining water.

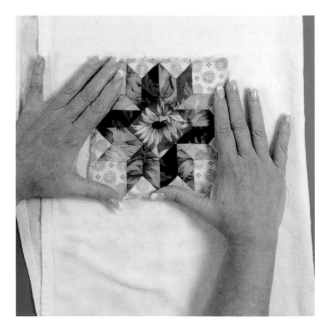

Smooth the block out on the towel and let dry before removing the paper templates.

TIP

Place several completed blocks in a sink of warm water before going to bed and remove them in the morning. If you are afraid the fabrics may bleed, add a color grabber sheet.

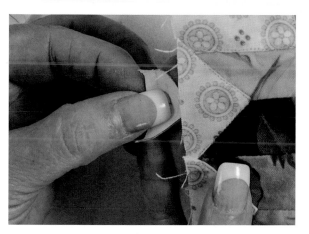

Pull out the paper templates along the raw edges of the block. If necessary, run the seams under water to flush out any remaining glue.

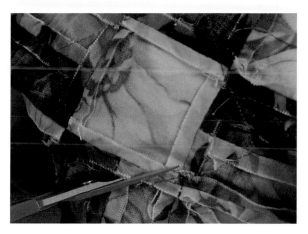

To remove inside templates, slit or cut the background fabric. Avoid cutting through the appliquéd stitches

Remove the inside paper templates. Cut away any excess fabric if you are going to hand appliqué or the foundation block will shadow through the completed block.

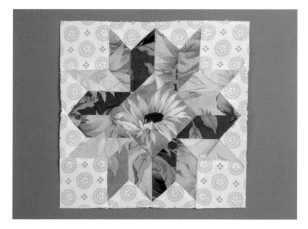

Smooth the block out again and press.

TIP

Press the seams open when sewing your foundation block to evenly distribute the bulk of the fabric in the seam allowance.

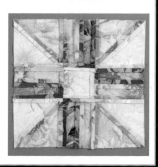

TIP

Press your appliquéd blocks on a folded bath towel. The towel absorbs the seams so that there is no "shadow" created by the seams on the front of the piece. Spray each piece with spray starch and press the wrong side to guarantee that all of the seams are pressed correctly. Then press the right side. The spray starch gives it a crisp look, reduces distortion and fraying, and protects the finished block.

The Pieced Appliqué™ Blocks

Liberty Star
6-1/2" Foundation Block

CUTTING THE PAPER TEMPLATES

Cut one of Templates A, B, C, D, E, F, and G on pages 25-27.

Template F is reverse appliquéd. Therefore, you must cut out the center circle. Because this appliqué touches the finished edge of the block on all four sides, this template includes the seam allowance.

Template G (the star shape) is used for placement only.

> *Note: By reverse appliquéing the star points, it is possible to get sharp, precise points every time.*

The paper templates are glued to the wrong side of the fabric. Therefore, the turned appliqué is a mirror image of the original template. In this case, the A & B templates and the C & D templates are mirror images of each other. The templates provided have been reversed for you.

> *Note: If you are going to machine appliqué the block, see instructions on page 15. These instructions are written for hand appliqué.*

PIECING

This block consists of 7 pieces.

1   Cut the 6-1/2" foundation square from the medium print fabric.

2   Glue the A, B, C, D, and E paper templates to the wrong side of a scrap of light print fabric. Trim the fabric EXACTLY 1/4" away from the sides of each template. Turn the sides that form the star. They are marked with an * on the templates.

FABRICS

Light Print Fabric:
Scraps to Cut 1 of
Appliqué A, B, C, D, & E

Medium Print Fabric:
6-1/2" Square

Dark Print Fabric:
Scrap to Cut 1 of Appliqué F

Refer to General Instructions on pages 10-19 before beginning this block.

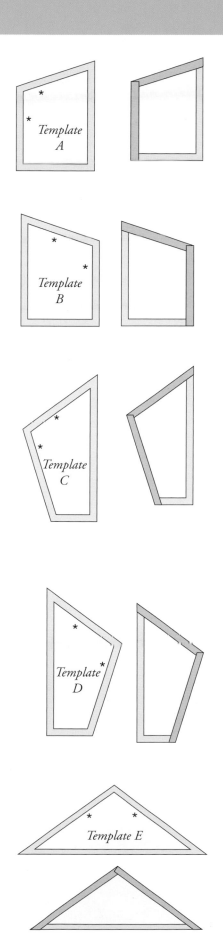

Template A

Template B

Template C

Template D

Template E

3 Center and glue the G paper template in place on the right side of the 6-1/2" medium print square. The top point of the star should be centered and placed 1/4" away from the top edge of the square. This template is used to aid in placement only. It will be removed when the A, B, C, D, and E appliqués are glued in place.

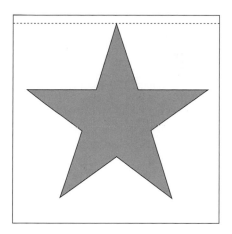

4 Glue the wrong side of the A, B, C, D, and E appliqués in place on the right side of the 6-1/2" medium print square. The turned sides of the appliqués should be placed even with the G paper template. Remove the G template.

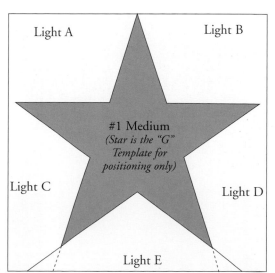

Light A   Light B

#1 Medium
*(Star is the "G"
Template for
positioning only)*

Light C   Light D

Light E

5 Glue the F paper template to the wrong side of a scrap of dark print fabric. Trim the fabric 1/4" away from the inner circle of the template. Trim the fabric even with the outer edge of the template—the outer seam allowance has been included in this template. Clip and turn the inner circle.

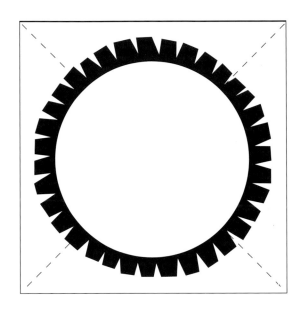

6 Glue the wrong side of the F appliqué in place on the right side of the 6-1/2" medium print square. The raw edges of the appliqué should be placed even with the raw edges of the medium print square.

7 Appliqué in place, leaving the raw edges open. Follow directions on pages 18-19 to remove paper templates and glue. Press.

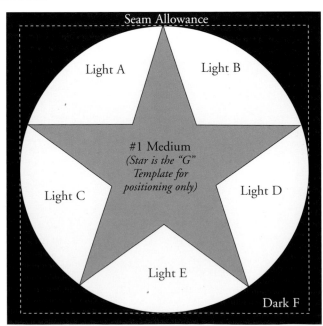

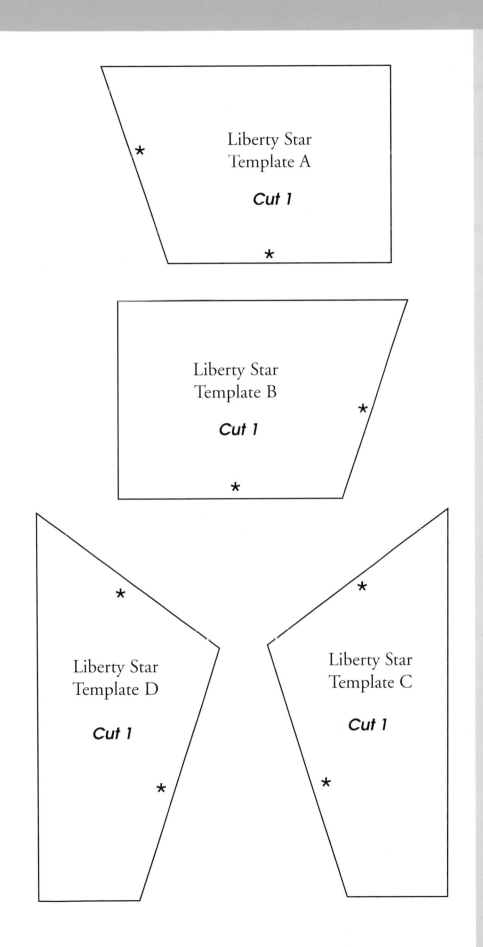

Liberty Star
Template A

Cut 1

Liberty Star
Template B

Cut 1

Liberty Star
Template D

Cut 1

Liberty Star
Template C

Cut 1

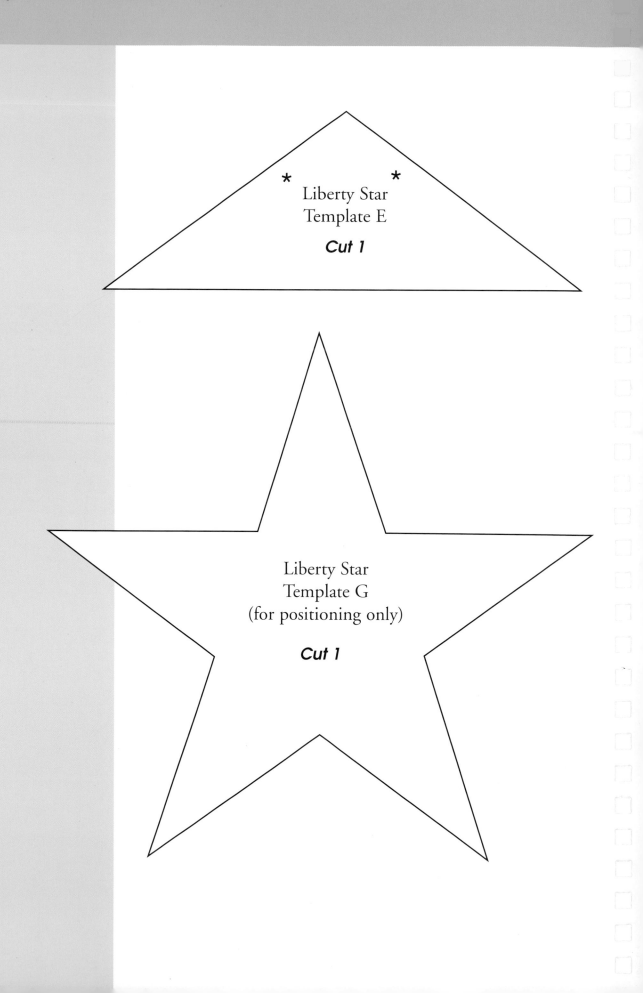

* *
Liberty Star
Template E

Cut 1

Liberty Star
Template G
(for positioning only)

Cut 1

Liberty Star Template F

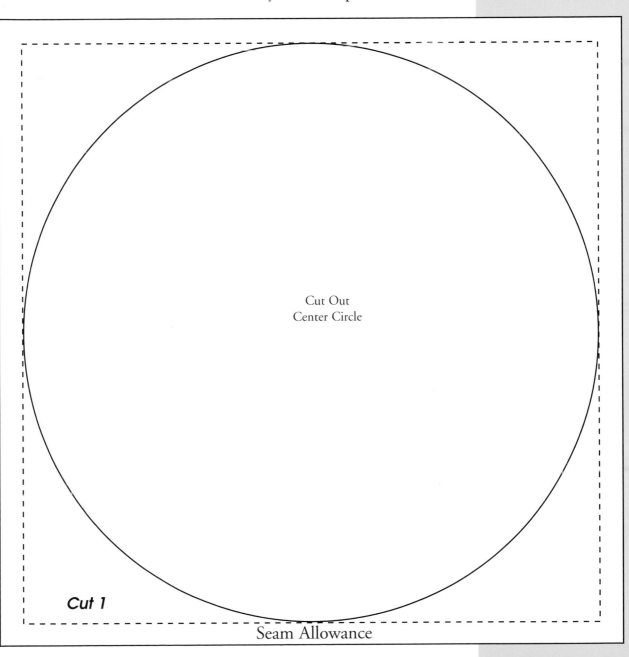

Cut Out
Center Circle

Cut 1

Seam Allowance

FABRICS

Light Print Fabric:
6-1/2" Square

Medium Print Fabric:
Scraps to Cut 4 of Appliqué B

Dark Print Fabric:
Scraps to Cut 4 of Appliqué C
& 4 of Appliqué D

Floral Fabric:
Scrap to Fussy Cut 1 of Appliqué A

*Refer to General Instructions on pages 10-19
before beginning this block.*

Homemaker

6-1/2" Foundation Block

CUTTING THE PAPER TEMPLATES

Cut one of Template A and four of Templates B, C,
and D on page 30.

> **Note:** *The paper templates are glued to
> the wrong side of the fabric. Therefore, the
> turned appliqué is a mirror image of the
> original template. In this case, the C & D
> templates are mirror images of each other.
> The templates have been reversed for you.*
> **Note:** *If you are going to machine appliqué
> the block, see instructions on page 15. These
> instructions are written for hand appliqué.*

PIECING
This block consists of 14 pieces.

1 Cut the 6-1/2" square from the light
print fabric.

2 Glue the A paper template to the wrong side
of a scrap of floral fabric. Place the template
so that a flower is centered in the appliqué.
Trim the fabric 1/4" away from the template
on all sides. Turn all sides.

3 Glue the B paper templates to the wrong
side of a scrap of medium print fabric. Trim
the fabric exactly 1/4" away from the straight
sides of each template. Do not turn these
sides. Trim the fabric approximately 1/4" away
from the curved edge of each template. Turn
the curved edge.
Note: ★ *on paper templates indicates sides
of fabric to be turned.*

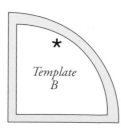 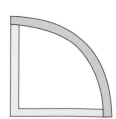

4 Glue the C and D paper templates to the wrong side of a scrap of dark print fabric. Trim the fabric exactly 1/4" away from the straight sides of each template. Do not turn the straight sides. Trim the fabric approximately 1/4" away from the two curved edges. Turn the long curved edge.

Template C

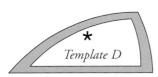

Template D

5 Glue the C and D appliqués in place on the B appliqué. The turned, long curved edges should be placed on the dashed lines of the B template. Turn the short curved edges of the C and D appliqués OVER the top edge of the B appliqué.

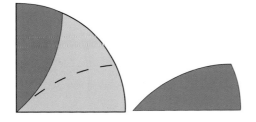

6 With a water soluble marker, draw a vertical and horizontal line on the 6-1/2" light print square (3-1/4" away from each edge). Glue the A appliqué in place. Each corner of the appliqué should touch the drawn lines.

7 Glue the other appliqués in place. The raw edges of the appliqués should be placed even with the raw edges of the 6-1/2" light print square.

8 Appliqué in place, leaving the raw edges open. Follow directions on pages 18-19 to remove paper templates and glue. Press.

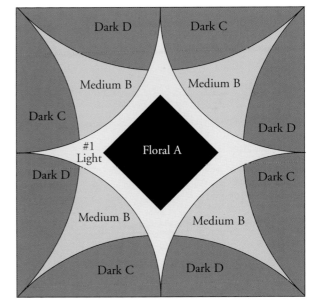

Dark D | Dark C

Medium B | Medium B

Dark C

Dark D

#1 Light | Floral A

Dark D | Dark C

Medium B | Medium B

Dark C | Dark D

Homemaker
Template A

*

Cut 1

*

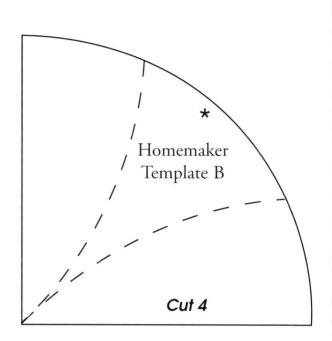

Homemaker
Template B

*

Cut 4

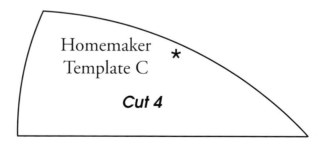

Homemaker
Template C *

Cut 4

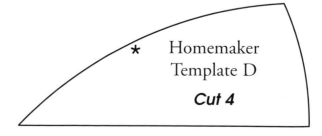

* Homemaker
Template D

Cut 4

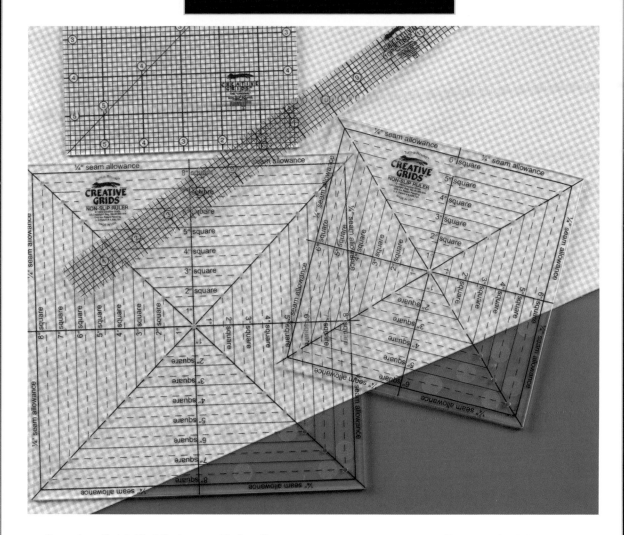

Creative Grids™ Miniature Ruler Set

The 6" square ruler in this set has 1/8" solid lines which make it easy to cut small pieces accurately. The diagonal line on the ruler is great for trimming half-square triangles.

Add A-Quarter™ Ruler

This ruler, which was actually designed for paper-piecing, has a 1/4" raised lip along one side. Butt this lip along the edge of a template to rotary cut a perfect 1/4" seam allowance every time.

Creative Grids™ *Square It Up & Fussy Cut* Rulers

Designed to complement the Pieced Appliqué™ blocks in this book, these rulers are available in 6-1/2", 8-1/2", 9-1/2", and 12-1/2" squares. Use them to square up a block by placing the correct size of the ruler over the block to be trimmed. Match the horizontal, vertical, and diagonal lines with the seam lines of the block. The 1/4" seam is marked on the entire outside edge of the ruler so the points of your triangles won't be cut off.

The 6-1/2" square ruler was used for the Pieced Appliqué™ blocks. The 8-1/2" square ruler was used in making the pieced setting blocks in the finished quilt.

See page 33 to learn how to use the fussy cutting aspect of this ruler.

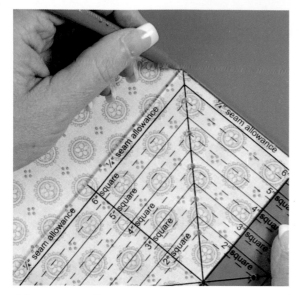

MARK THE FOUNDATION BLOCK

Use a water soluble marker to draw a vertical and horizontal line 3-1/4" away from each side of the foundation block.

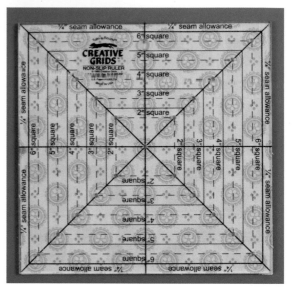

CHECK THE MARKED LINES

Place the 6-1/2" ruler on the fabric square to be sure your marked lines are centered correctly. The appliqués will be aligned with the markings, so they need to be accurate.

LAYERING THE APPLIQUÉS

Glue the wrong side of appliqués C and D. Place on the right side of appliqué B. Turn the short curved edges of the C and D appliqués over the top edge of the B appliqué.

GLUE THE APPLIQUÉS IN PLACE

Glue the layered appliqués in place on the foundation block. The raw edges of the appliqués should be placed even with the raw edges of the foundation block.

Technique Notebook

The center appliqué in the Homemaker block was fussy cut to showcase a sunflower. This technique can be used on many of the Pieced Appliqué™ blocks to add a dramatic effect.

Choose a Design and Mark the Fabric

When fussy cutting an appliqué, as in the Homemaker block, measure your template to determine what size to cut your fabric. Place the ruler over the design you have chosen and mark the fabric.

As shown in the inset, the *Square It Up & Fussy Cut* rulers have holes where a fabric marker can be used. This guarantees a centered design every time.

Connect the Dots and Cut

Remove the ruler and use it to draw lines that connect the dots on the fabric. Cut out the fussy cut design. Your design is perfectly centered.

Place the Fussy Cut Appliqué

After gluing the paper template onto the fussy cut fabric and turning the sides, it is placed in the center of the foundation block. Each corner of the appliqué should touch the previously drawn lines.

Cross Roads

6-1/2" Foundation Block

CUTTING THE PAPER TEMPLATES

Cut two of Template A and four of Template B.

> **Note:** *Template B is a gentle curve so if the straight edges of the template are placed on the straight of grain, the curved sides will automatically be placed on the bias and may not have to be clipped.*
>
> **Note:** *If you are going to machine appliqué the block, see instructions on page 15. These instructions are written for hand appliqué.*

PIECING

This block consists of 7 pieces.

1 Glue the A paper templates to the wrong side of a scrap of the medium print fabric. Trim the fabric 1/4" away from the template on all sides. Turn the two long sides of each appliqué.
Note: *★ on paper templates indicates sides of fabric to be turned.*

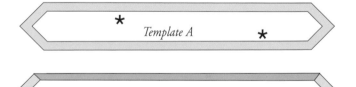

2 Glue the B paper templates to the wrong side of a scrap of the dark print fabric. Trim the fabric 1/4" away from the templates on all sides. Turn the two curved sides of each appliqué.

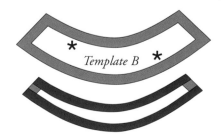

FABRICS

Light Print Fabric:
6-1/2" Square

Medium Print Fabric:
Scraps to Cut 2 of Appliqué A

Dark Print Fabric:
Scraps to Cut 4 of Appliqué B

Refer to General Instructions on pages 10-19 before beginning this block.

3 Center and diagonally place the A appliqués on the 6-1/2" light print square. The raw edges of the appliqués should be placed even with the raw edges of the square.

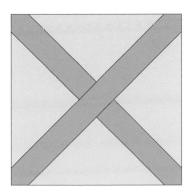

4 Place the B appliqués on top of the A appliqués. The raw edges of the appliqués should be placed even with the raw edges of the square.

5 Appliqué in place, leaving raw edges open. Follow directions on pages 18-19 to remove paper templates and glue. Press.

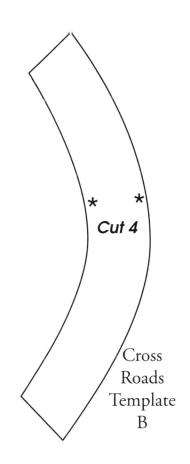

Cut 4

Cross Roads Template B

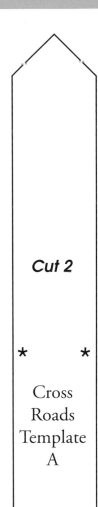

Cut 2

Cross Roads Template A

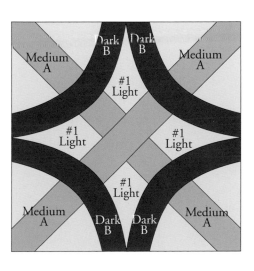

Four-Patch Foundation Block

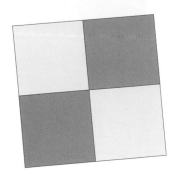

A four-patch is a block that consists of four squares of equal size. All of the four-patches in this book were made using this method.

Two squares of contrasting fabrics will make two four-patches. The squares must be cut at least 1" larger than the finished size of the block.

If you need a 6" finished four-patch, for instance, cut the squares at least 7". After sewing, the four-patches should measure 6-1/2". This includes the seam allowances.

I prefer to cut the squares 2" larger so that I can trim the four-patches to the correct size after the sewing is complete. In some cases, they are cut even larger so appliqués can be cut from the pieced block.

FABRICS

Cut 1—8" Square of
a Light Fabric

Cut 1—8" Square of
a Dark Fabric

PIECING

1 Place the light fabric square, right sides together, on top of the dark fabric square.

Note: Use spray starch to iron the squares together.

2 Sew a 1/4" seam along two opposite sides of the squares using a matching cotton thread. Clip all threads.

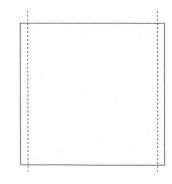

3 Cut this unit in half, parallel to the sewn seams. Each strip should measure 4". Press the seams open.

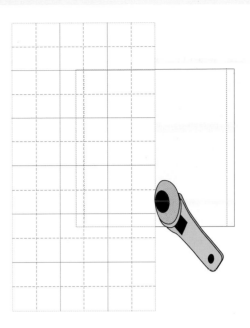

4 Place these two units, right sides together, with the dark fabric strip on top of the light fabric strip. Match the seams.

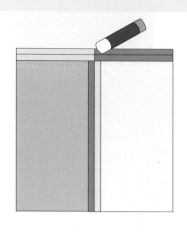

5 To ensure the center seams of the four-patches match perfectly, place a dab of glue to hold them in place. Fold back the top unit about an inch and line up the seams. Do not place any glue 1/4" in from the edge or you will glue the seam allowance closed and will not be able to press it open later. Any dab of glue that shows on the front of the block will disappear when the templates are removed.

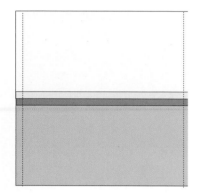

6 Sew a 1/4" seam along the two opposite sides that are perpendicular to the sewn seams.

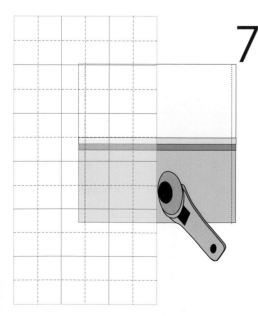

7 Cut this unit in half, parallel to the sewn seams. Each strip should measure 4". Press the seams open.

8 Place the 6-1/2" Creative Grids™ *Square It Up & Fussy Cut* ruler on top of the four-patch, placing the horizontal and vertical lines on the seam lines of the four-patch. Trim the outside edge of the block.

Note: *In most cases, one four-patch will be used as the foundation block and will be trimmed to 6-1/2". Trim the one with the perfect center. Appliqués will be cut from the other four-patch, so the center will be cut away. Do NOT trim the second four-patch. It is over-sized so that the appliqués can be cut from it.*

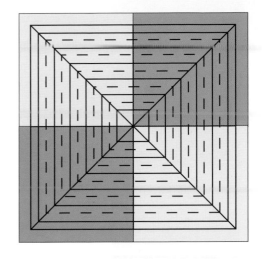

You now have two completed four-patch units.

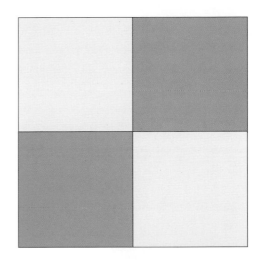

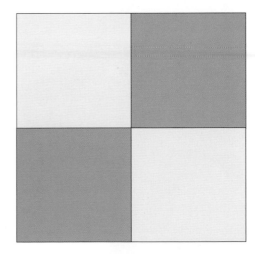

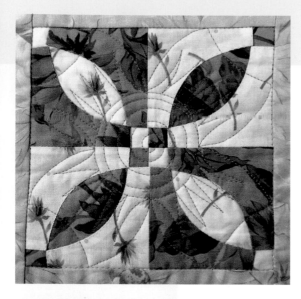

True Lover's Knot

Four-Patch Foundation Block

CUTTING THE PAPER TEMPLATE

Cut four of Template A.
The fabric for the A appliqués will be cut from one of the four-patches.

> **Note:** *By placing and cutting the A templates from a pieced four-patch block, the raw edge of the appliqué is on the straight of the grain of the fabric so the finished block is more stable. The curved edges of the templates are automatically placed on the bias of the fabric. Therefore, you may be able to turn these curves without clipping the fabric.*
>
> *The fabrics for two of the appliqués are mirror images of the other two appliqués. Since the appliqués are cut from a completed four-patch, these are automatically reversed for you.*
>
> *Only one center of a four-patch will show in the finished block, so save the "best" four-patch for the foundation block.*

PIECING

This block consists of 8 pieces.

1. Following the four-patch foundation block directions on page 36, make two four-patches with the #1 light print square and the #2 dark print square. The finished four-patches are over-sized. They should measure approximately 8".

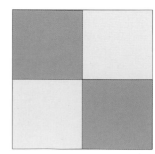

2 Glue the A templates to the wrong side of a four-patch, placing them at least 1/4" away from the outer edge of the four-patch. Match the drawn line on the templates to the seam line on the four-patch.

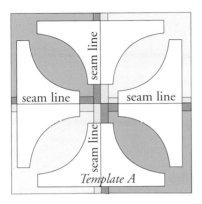

3 Trim the fabric EXACTLY 1/4" away from the straight sides of each template. Trim the fabric approximately 1/4" away from the curved edges. Do not turn the long straight side of each template. Turn all other edges. Two appliqués will have the light fabric on the left and two will have the light fabric on the right.

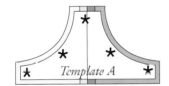 

4 Trim the remaining four-patch to 6-1/2" (3-1/4" from each seam).

5 Glue the wrong side of the appliqués in place on the trimmed four-patch, matching the seam lines and alternating the fabrics. The raw edges of the appliqués should be placed even with the raw edges of the trimmed four-patch.

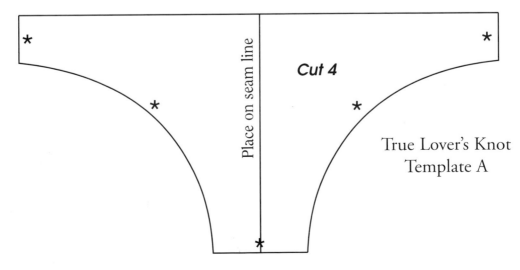

6 Appliqué in place. Follow directions on pages 18-19 to remove paper templates and glue. Press.

Place on seam line

Cut 4

True Lover's Knot
Template A

Kansas Dug-Out

Four-Patch Foundation Block

CUTTING THE PAPER TEMPLATES

Cut five of Template A and four of Templates B and C.

> **Note:** *By appliquéing the A, B, and C templates, there are no inset points.*
>
> *None of the centers of the four-patches will show in the finished block, so if the seams don't match perfectly, don't worry about it. They will be covered by the A appliqués.*
>
> *Fussy cutting these appliqués can make a dramatic difference in the finished block.*

PIECING

This block consists of 29 pieces.

1 Following the four-patch foundation block directions on page 36, make four four-patches with the #1 light print squares and the #2 medium print squares. The finished four-patches are over-sized, they should measure approximately 4".

2 Trim the four-patches to 3-1/2" (1-3/4" from the center seam).

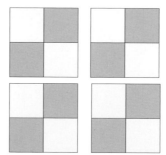

3 Sew together the four four-patches to form a sixteen-patch, alternating fabrics. These seams show so they must match. Press the seams open.

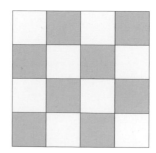

4 Glue the A, B, and C templates to the wrong side of a scrap of dark print fabric.

5 Trim the fabric EXACTLY 1/4" away from the templates on all sides. Turn all sides of the A appliqués, the two short sides of the B appliqués, and the long side of the C appliqués.

Note: ★ *on paper templates indicates sides of fabric to be turned.*

6 Glue the wrong side of the appliqués in place on the pieced sixteen-patch block.

7 Appliqué in place. Follow directions on pages 18-19 to remove paper templates and glue. Press.

Template A

Template B

Template C

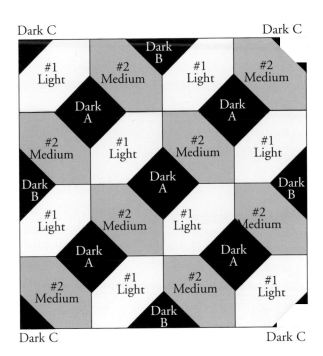

Kansas Dug-Out Templates

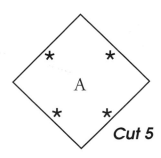
A — Cut 5

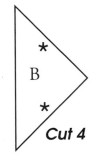
B — Cut 4

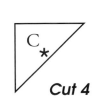
C — Cut 4

Nine-Patch Foundation Block

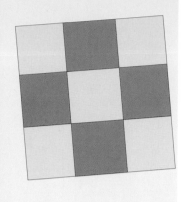

A nine-patch block traditionally consists of nine squares sewn in three rows of three squares. In this book, a nine-patch consists of three rows of three units. Those nine units may consist of rectangles, half-square triangles, and even nine-patches. The method is the same.

Make a sample block to learn the technique before cutting the fabric for your quilt. Measure the completed block to check your seam allowance.

The completed block should measure 6-1/2".

FABRICS

5—2-1/2" Squares of Light Fabric

4—2-1/2" Squares of Dark Fabric

PIECING

1 Lay out the nine squares in three rows of three blocks each. In this example, the light fabric squares are placed at the corners and in the center. Follow each Pieced Appliqué™ block's directions for fabric placement.

2 Place the squares in the center column – right sides together on the squares in the left-hand column. Pick up the first pair in the top left corner. Then, pick up the middle pair, then the bottom pair. The bottom pair of squares will be on the bottom of the stack. Pick up the right-hand column of squares from the top to the bottom in the same manner.

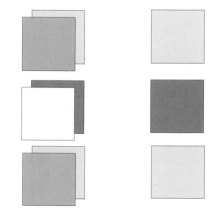

3 Pick up the top two squares, which are already right sides together, and sew the right side of the squares. Do not break the thread. Pick up the next two squares and sew the right side of these squares. Do not break the thread. Pick up the last two squares that are right sides together and sew the right side of these squares. Three squares will be left. The top square will be right side up. You have sewn three sets of two squares that are held together by threads.

4 Open the first set of squares and place the top, light square, right sides together, on the dark fabric square. Sew on the right side of the square. Do not break the thread.

5 Open the second set of squares and place the next, dark square, right sides together, on the light fabric square. Sew on the right side of the square. Do not break the thread.

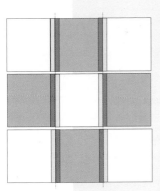

6 Open the third set of squares and place the remaining light square, right sides together, on the dark fabric square. Sew on the right side of the square. Do not clip the thread. The threads will hold the rows together so you don't lose any pieces and act as pins when sewing the rows togther. Press the seams open.

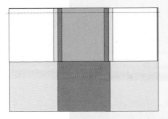

7 Place the second row, right sides together, on the first row, matching the seams. Place a dab of glue on these seams so everything matches perfectly. Place the third row, right sides together, on the second row. Match the seams and sew this seam.

8 Clip the threads that held the rows together and press the seams open.

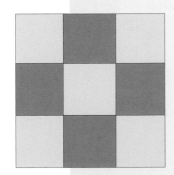

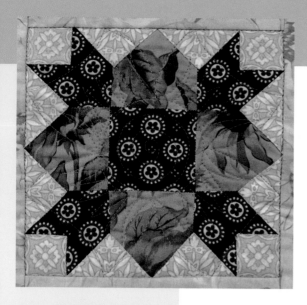

Weathervane

Nine-Patch Foundation Block

CUTTING THE PAPER TEMPLATES

Cut eight of Template A and four of Template B.

Note: *Fussy cutting the center square and the appliqués will add drama to this block.*

PIECING

This block consists of 21 pieces.

1 Following the nine-patch foundation block directions on page 44, make a nine-patch with the #2 dark print squares (center and corners) and the #1 medium print squares. Press the seams open.

FABRICS

Light Print Fabric:
Scraps to Cut 8 of Appliqué A
& 4 of Appliqué B

Medium Print Fabric:
#1—Cut 4—2-1/2" Squares

Dark Print Fabric:
#2—Cut 5—2-1/2" Squares

Refer to General Instructions on pages 10-19 before beginning this block.

2 Glue the A paper templates to the wrong side of a scrap of light print fabric. Trim the fabric EXACTLY 1/4" away from the templates on all sides. Turn the two short sides of each appliqué.
Note: ⋆ *on paper templates indicates sides of fabric to be turned.*

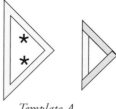

Template A

3 Glue the B paper templates to the wrong side of a scrap of light print fabric. Trim the fabric EXACTLY 1/4" away from each template on all sides. Turn two adjoining sides of each template.

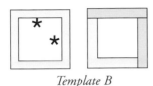

Template B

4 Glue the wrong side of the A appliqués in place on the pieced nine-patch block. Place the raw edges of the appliqués even with the raw edges of the block.

5 Glue the wrong side of the B appliqués in place on the pieced nine-patch block. Place the raw edges of the appliqués even with the raw edges of the block.

6 Appliqué in place, leaving raw edges open. Follow directions on pages 18-19 to remove paper templates and glue. Press.

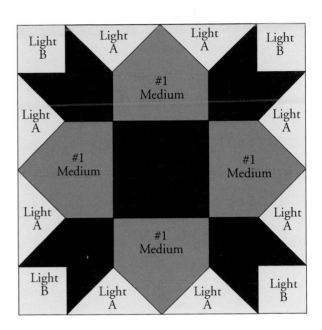

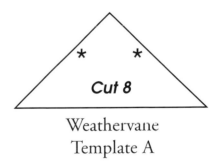

Cut 8

Weathervane
Template A

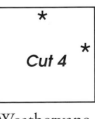

Cut 4

Weathervane
Template B

PLACE THE TRIANGLE APPLIQUÉS

Place the eight triangle appliqués on the nine-patch foundation block. Place the turned point of the triangle on the seam and the raw edge of the appliqué even with the raw edge of the foundation block. Glue the wrong side of the appliqué in place.

PLACE THE CORNER APPLIQUÉS

Place the four square appliqués on the corners of the nine-patch block. Place the raw edges of the appliqués even with the raw edges of the block. The square and triangle appliqués will overlap.

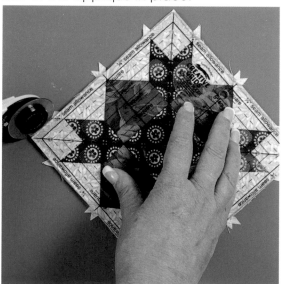

TRIM THE APPLIQUÉS

Place a 6-1/2" ruler on the block and using a rotary cutter, trim the tails of the triangle appliqués even with the pieced foundation block.

FINISH THE BLOCK

Hand or machine stitch the appliqués in place, leaving raw edges open. Remove the paper templates and glue, following the directions on pages 18-19.

Note: *I recommend using the versatile Creative Grids™ Square It Up & Fussy Cut ruler when building your Pieced Appliqué™ blocks.*

HIDING THE KNOT

Knots should be hidden beneath the appliqué piece. Do not place your knot on the wrong side of the foundation square. The thread tail could shadow through the finished block.

HAND STITCHING THE APPLIQUÉS

Hand stitch the turned edges of the appliqué, using an invisible appliqué stitch. Be careful to catch only the fabric when stitching, you don't want to sew the paper templates into your block. Leave the raw edges open.

MACHINE STITCHING THE APPLIQUÉS

When machine stitching your appliqué pieces, use a narrow zigzag stitch with invisible thread in the top of your machine and 50 or 60 weight thread in the bobbin.

ZIGZAG STITCH

Machine zigzag stitch only the turned edges of the appliqué. Leave the raw edges of the block unstitched. Remove the paper templates and glue, following the directions on pages 18-19. Press the block.

Cornerstone

Nine-Patch Foundation Block

CUTTING THE PAPER TEMPLATES

Cut four of Template A and four of Template B.

> **Note:** *Fussy cutting the center square will add drama to this block.*

PIECING

This block consists of 17 pieces.

> **Note:** *The paper templates are glued to the wrong side of the fabric. The templates have been reversed for you.*

1 Following the the nine-patch foundation block directions on page 44, make a nine-patch with the #1 light print squares (corners); the #3 floral print square (center); and the #2 medium print squares. Press the seams open.

FABRICS

Light Print Fabric:
#1—Cut 4—2-1/2" Squares

Medium Print Fabric:
#2—Cut 4—2-1/2" Squares

Floral Print Fabric:
#3—Cut 1—2-1/2" Square

Dark Print Fabric:
Scraps to Cut 4 of Appliqué A
& 4 of Appliqué B

Refer to General Instructions on pages 10-19 before beginning this block.

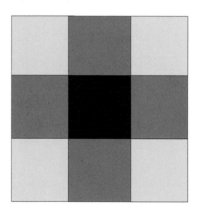

2 Glue the A paper templates to the wrong side of a scrap of dark print fabric. Trim the fabric EXACTLY 1/4" away from the templates on all sides. Turn the two sides of each appliqué marked with an * on the template. Do not turn the other sides. Glue the wrong side of the appliqués in place on the pieced nine-patch block. Place the raw edge of the appliqués even with the raw edge of the block.

> **Note:** *★ on paper templates indicates sides of fabric to be turned.*

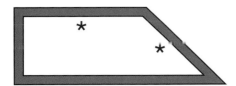

Template A

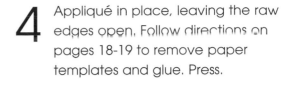

4 Appliqué in place, leaving the raw edges open. Follow directions on pages 18-19 to remove paper templates and glue. Press.

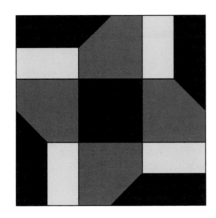

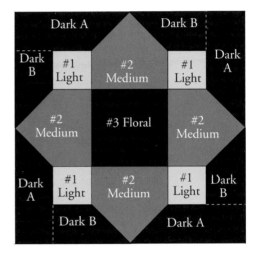

3 Glue the B paper templates to the wrong side of a scrap of dark print fabric. Trim the fabric EXACTLY 1/4" away from the templates on all sides. Turn the three shortest sides of each appliqué marked with an * on the template. Do not turn the longest side. Glue the wrong side of the appliqués in place on the nine-patch foundation block.

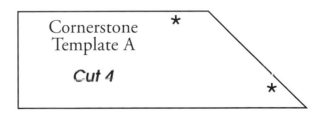

Cornerstone Template A

Cut 4

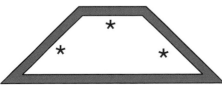

Cornerstone Template B

Cut 4

Template B

51

Christmas Star

Nine-Patch Foundation Block

Cutting the Paper Templates

Cut four of Templates A and B.

Piecing

This block consists of 17 pieces.

> **Note:** The center 3-1/2" cut square is a great place to fussy cut a beautiful fabric.

1 Following the nine-patch foundation block directions on page 44, make a nine-patch with the #2 medium print square (center); the #1 light print squares (corners); and the #3 dark print rectangles. Press the seams open.

Fabrics

Light Print Fabric:
#1—Cut 4—2" Squares
Scraps to Cut 4 of Appliqué A

Medium Print Fabric:
#2—Cut 1—3-1/2" Square
Scraps to Cut 4 of Appliqué B

Dark Print Fabric:
#3—Cut 4—2" x 3-1/2" Rectangles

Refer to General Instructions on pages 10-19 before beginning this block.

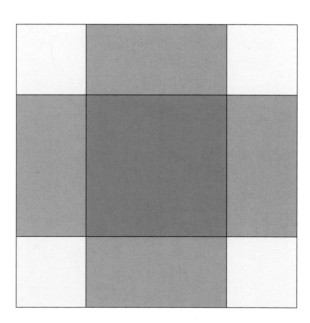

> **Note:** If you are going to machine appliqué the block, see instructions on page 15. These instructions are written for hand appliqué.

2 Glue the A paper templates to the wrong side of a scrap of light print fabric. Place the longest side of the A templates on the straight of grain. Trim the fabric 1/4" away from the templates on all sides. Turn the two short sides. Do not turn the longest side.

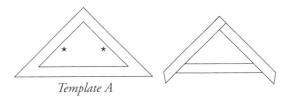

Template A

3 Glue the B paper templates to the wrong side of a scrap of medium print fabric. Trim the fabric 1/4" away from the templates on all sides. Turn two adjoining sides. Place a B appliqué on top of the turned sides of an A appliqué and turn the two remaining sides of the B appliqué over the A appliqué. Make a total of four of these units.

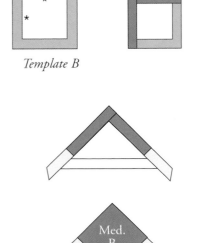

Template B

4 Glue the wrong side of the appliqués in place on the foundation block. The raw edges of the appliqués should be placed even with the raw edges of the block.

5 Appliqué in place, leaving raw edges open. Follow directions on pages 18-19 to remove paper templates and glue. Press.

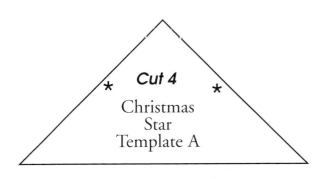

Cut 4
Christmas
Star
Template A

★ Cut 4 ★
Christmas
Star
Template B

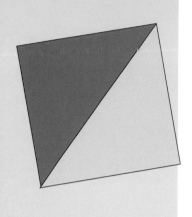

A half-square triangle is a square that consists of two ninety-degree triangles pieced on the longest side. These half-square triangles can be made using two different methods.

If the half-square triangles need to be trimmed to a different size, I use Method #1.

If the finished size of the square is 3" – 3-1/2" including the seam allowance – I use Triangles on a Roll™ paper – Method #2.

METHOD #1:

Note: *Generally, when making half-square triangles, the squares should be cut 7/8" larger than the finished block. Since you are sewing bias seams, the sewing and pressing tend to distort the shape of your finished square. Therefore, I add 2" so that I can square them up to the correct size after stitching and pressing.*

FABRICS

2—4" Squares of Light Fabric

2—4" Squares of Dark Fabric

Make a sample block to learn the technique before cutting the fabric for your quilt.

In the Farmer's Daughter block on page 58, the half-square triangles were made from 4" squares and trimmed to 2-7/8". In the following example, the fabric is cut and trimmed as if you were making that block.

PIECING

1. Place a light fabric square, right sides together, on top of a dark fabric square. Draw a line across the diagonal. Be sure to use a pencil or a marking tool that is water soluble. Ink may bleed onto your quilt when you wash it. Repeat with the other set of squares.
   Note: *It is easier to draw the line from the center out in both directions so you don't wrinkle the corners.*

2 Stitch a seam 1/4" on each side of the drawn line. Cut on the drawn line. Repeat with the other set of squares.

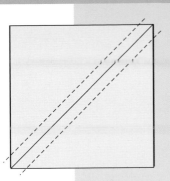

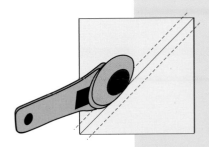

3 Open the half-square triangles and press the seams open. Each set of squares will make two half-square triangle units. These blocks will be slightly larger than 3-1/2".

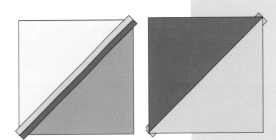

4 Place the 6" Miniature Ruler on the upper left corner of the right side of the square. The diagonal line marking on the ruler should be placed on the seam line. Trim the top and left side.

5 Turn the block so the uncut edges are on the top and left side. Place the 6" Miniature Ruler so the diagonal line is placed on the seam line and the 2-7/8" markings are even with the square on the right and bottom sides. Trim the top and left side. The finished square now measures to 2-7/8".

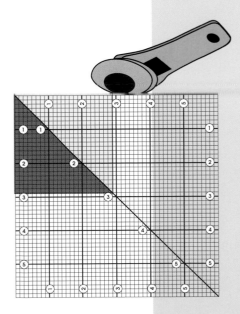

Half-Square Triangles Foundation Block

FABRICS

1—4-1/2" x 8-1/2" Rectangle of Light Fabric

1—4-1/2" x 8-1/2" Rectangle of Dark Fabric

1—Rectangle of Two Squares of 3" Triangles on a Roll™ paper

METHOD #2—Using Triangles on a Roll™ paper:
PIECING

1 Place the 4-1/2" x 8-1/2" rectangle of light fabric on the 4-1/2" x 8-1/2" rectangle of dark fabric, right sides together. Pin the triangle paper to the fabric avoiding any printed lines. Sew on all of the dashed lines.

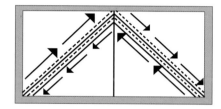

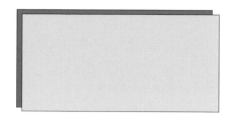

2 Cut on all of the solid lines, including the outside edges. You have made 4 half-square triangles. DO NOT REMOVE THE PAPER.

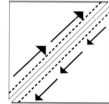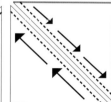

3 Place the paper side down on the ironing board and press all of the seams toward the dark fabric. The paper stabilizes the bias seam so it does not become distorted while you are pressing. Repeat for all four half-square triangles.

4 Trim the "tails" that stick out past the square. Remove the paper by tearing it out in both directions from the center point. Do not try to tear it away from the seamed corners or you could tear out a few of the stitches and weaken your final block. Repress the seams open. Repeat for all four half-square triangles.

FUSSY CUTTING

Many of the appliqués can be fussy cut to showcase a particular design in the fabric. This technique adds drama and eye appeal to the Pieced Appliqué™ blocks.

The Creative Grids™ *Square It Up & Fussy Cut* ruler makes the process quick and easy. This ruler consists of squares drawn symmetrically around a center hole. These symmetrical squares are drawn with solid black lines at 1" increments. Squares are drawn with black dashed lines at the 1/2" increments starting with 1-1/2". Holes are drilled at the center and at the corners of the dashed squares drawn at the 1/2" increments beginning with the 1-1/2" square.

These holes are drilled so that a water soluble pen tip can be inserted to mark the fabric underneath. By marking the fabric through these holes, a 1/4" seam allowance is automatically added to the piece.

PLACE THE RULER AND MARK YOUR FABRIC

Place the ruler over the design you want to fussy cut. In this case, the ruler is placed over a sunflower. The sunflower is centered within the 2" solid black square. A blue water soluble marker is used to mark the corner of the dashed square at 2-1/2". This automatically adds the seam allowance to that piece. When cut, the sunflower will be in the exact center of the square.

ADD THE PAPER TEMPLATE
The fussy cut square is now ready to have the paper template glued to the wrong side of the fabric.

FUSSY CUT THE DESIGN
Remove the ruler and use it to draw lines that connect the marked dots on the fabric. Cut out the fabric square on the drawn line.

TIP
Triangles can be fussy cut by marking the corner and points of the triangle. Trim the two straight sides; cut the diagonal.

FABRICS

Light Print Fabric:
Scraps to Cut 4 of Appliqué A
& 4 of Appliqué B

Medium Print Fabric:
#1—Cut 1—1-3/4" Square
#2—Cut 2—4" Squares

Medium Dark Print Fabric
#3—Cut 2—4" Squares

Dark Print Fabric:
#4—Cut 4—1-3/4" x 2-7/8"
Rectangles

*Refer to General Instructions on pages 10-19
before beginning this block.*

Farmer's Daughter

Half-Square Triangles Foundation Block

CUTTING THE PAPER TEMPLATES

Cut four of Templates A and B on page 60.

> **Note:** *Choose fabrics that will showcase the light, medium, and dark aspects of the design.*

PIECING

This block consists of 21 pieces.

1. Using Method #1 on page 54, make four half-square triangles with the #2 medium print fabric and the #3 medium dark print fabric. Press the seams open. Trim the finished half-square triangles to 2-7/8".

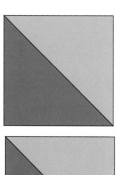

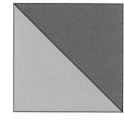

2 Following the nine-patch foundation block directions on page 44, make a nine-patch with the #1 medium print square (center); the trimmed half-square triangles (corners); and the #4 dark print rectangles. Press the seams open.

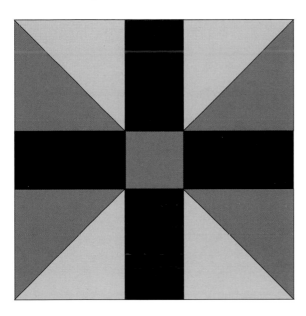

3 Glue the A paper templates to the wrong side of a scrap of light print fabric. Trim the fabric EXACTLY 1/4" away from all sides of the templates. Turn two adjoining sides of the appliqués.
Note: ★ *on paper templates indicates sides of fabric to be turned.*

Template A

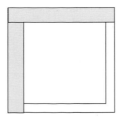

4 Glue the wrong side of the appliqués in place on the pieced half-square triangles. The raw edge of the appliqués should be placed even with the raw edge of the corners of the half-square triangles.

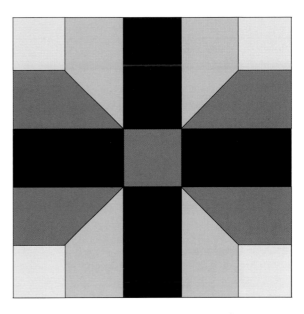

5 Glue the B paper templates to the wrong side of a scrap of light print fabric. Trim the fabric EXACTLY 1/4" away from all sides of the templates. Turn the three short sides.

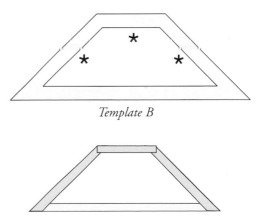

Template B

Farmer's Daughter continued

6 Glue the wrong side of the appliqués in place on the pieced block. The raw edges of the appliqués should be placed even with the raw edges of the pieced block.

7 Appliqué in place, leaving the raw edges open. Follow directions on pages 18-19 to remove paper templates and glue. Press.

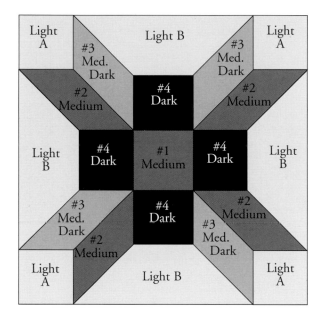

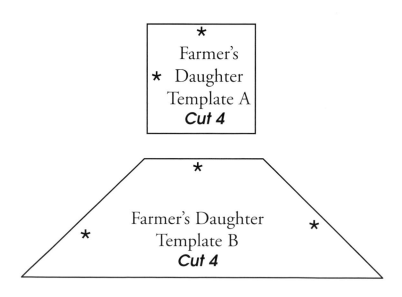

TRIMMING HALF-SQUARE TRIANGLES

Follow Method #1 on page 56 to make the number of half-square triangles needed for your block. To trim the half-square triangles to the size required, follow the example in the steps below.

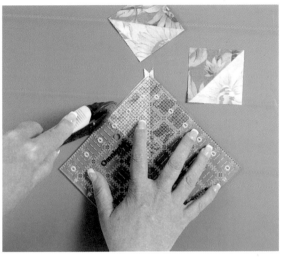

MAKING HALF-SQUARE TRIANGLES

The half-square triangles in the example above are slightly larger than 3-1/2". They need to be trimmed to 2-7/8".

PLACE THE RULER AND TRIM TWO SIDES

Place the ruler on the upper left corner of the right side of the square. The diagonal line marking on the ruler should be placed on the seam line. Trim the top and left side.

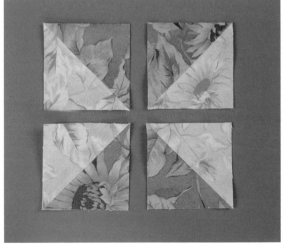

TRIM THE REMAINING TWO SIDES

Turn the block so the uncut edges are on the top and left side. Place the ruler so the diagonal line is placed on the seam line and the 2-7/8" markings are even with the square on the right and bottom sides. Trim the top and left side.

FINISHED HALF-SQUARE TRIANGLES

The finished half-square triangles should now measure 2-7/8" and are ready to be pieced into your foundation block.

Laurel's Wreath

Half-Square Triangles Foundation Block

CUTTING THE PAPER TEMPLATES

Cut four of Template A, eight of Template B, and one of Template C on page 65.

> **Note:** *Choose fabrics that will showcase the light, medium, and dark aspects of the design. You may also choose two different shades of one color for #2 and #3 and two shades of a different color for #4 and #5.*

PIECING

This block consists of 29 pieces.

1 Using Method #1 on page 54, make four half-square triangles with the #4 medium dark print fabric and the #5 dark print fabric. Press the seams open. Trim the finished half-square triangles to 2-3/4".

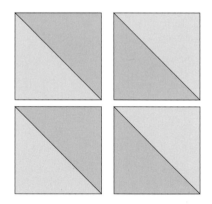

FABRICS

Light Print Fabric:
#1—Cut 1—2" Square
Scraps to Cut 4 of Appliqué A,
8 of Appliqué B, & 1 of Appliqué C

Medium Light Print Fabric:
#2—Cut 1—1-1/4" x 14" Strip

Medium Print Fabric:
#3—Cut 1—1-1/4" x 14" Strip

Medium Dark Print Fabric:
#4—Cut 2—3-1/2" Squares

Dark Print Fabric:
#5—Cut 2—3-1/2" Squares

Refer to General Instructions on pages 10-19 before beginning this block.

2 Sew a #2 medium light print fabric strip to a #3 medium print fabric strip along the 14" length of the strip. It should measure 2" x 14". It is longer than needed so you can straighten the ends before cutting the 2-3/4" units. Press the seam open. Cut this strip into four—2-3/4" units.

3 Following the nine-patch foundation block directions on page 44, make a nine-patch with the #1 light print square (center); the trimmed half-square triangles (corners); and the striped units completed in Step #2.

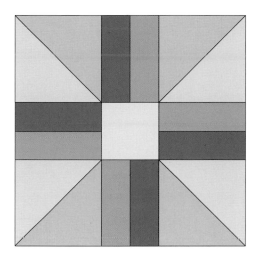

5 Glue the wrong side of the A appliqués in place on the pieced half-square triangles. The raw edge of the appliqués should be placed even with the raw edge of the corners of the half-square triangles.

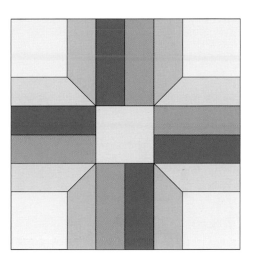

4 Glue the A paper templates to the wrong side of a scrap of light print fabric. Trim the fabric EXACTLY 1/4" away from all sides of the templates. Turn two adjoining sides of the appliqués.

Note: ★ *on paper templates indicates sides of fabric to be turned.*

Template A

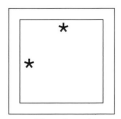

6 Glue the B paper templates to the wrong side of a scrap of light print fabric. Trim the fabric EXACTLY 1/4" away from all sides of the templates. Turn the two short sides.

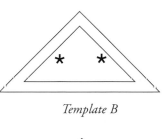

Template B

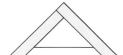

7   Glue the wrong side of the B appliqués in place on the pieced block. Place the turned points of the triangle appliqués on the seam lines. The raw edges of the appliqués should be placed even with the raw edge of the pieced block.

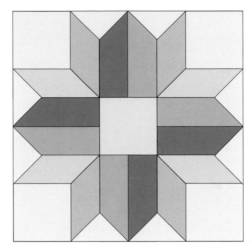

8   Glue the C paper template to the wrong side of a scrap of light print fabric. Trim the fabric EXACTLY 1/4" away from all sides of the template. Turn all sides.

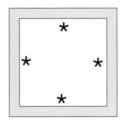

Template C

9   Glue the wrong side of the C appliqué in place on the pieced block. The corners of the appliqué should be placed on the seam of the striped units. The #1 light print square will be covered by this appliqué.

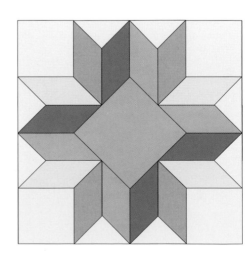

10 Appliqué in place, leaving the raw edges open. Follow directions on pages 18-19 to remove paper templates and glue. Press.

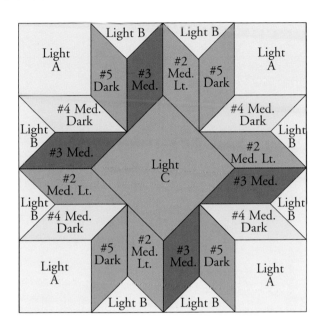

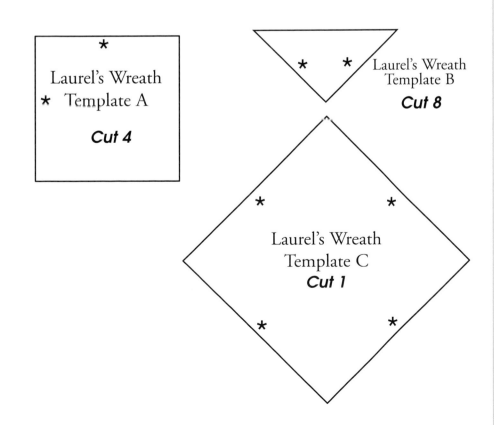

Pinwheel Foundation Block _____

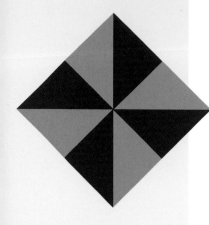

A pinwheel is made from four half-square triangles.

Make a sample block to learn the technique before cutting the fabric for your quilt.

PIECING

1 Using Method #2, page 58, make four half-square triangles with 3" Triangles on a Roll™ paper.

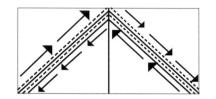

FABRICS

1—4-1/2" x 8-1/2" Rectangle of Light Fabric

1—4-1/2" x 8-1/2" Rectangle of Dark Fabric

1—Rectangle of Two Squares of 3" Triangles on a Roll™ paper

2 Lay out the four half-square triangles to form a pinwheel. It is possible to sew a mirror image of this block and have the blades of your pinwheel "blowing" in the other direction. Be careful.

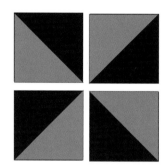

3 Place the half-square triangles in the second column, right sides together, over the first column, matching the seams. Place a dab of glue on the seam so it doesn't shift while sewing.

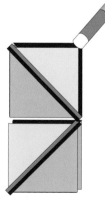

4 Sew these seams, one after the other, by chain-piecing them on the sewing machine.

5 Press the seams open. Check and make sure that the points of the triangles match 1/4" in from the outer edge. If they do not match now, the center of the pinwheel will not match after the final seam is sewn.

6 Place the right column over the left column, right sides together, matching the center seam. Use a dab of glue to make sure that nothing shifts when stitching. Sew this final seam. Press the seam open.

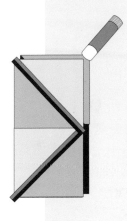

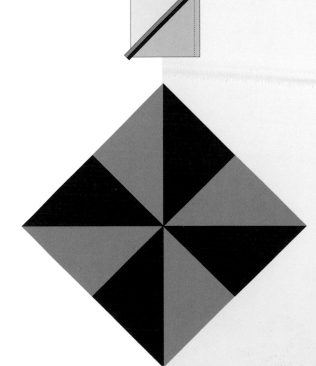

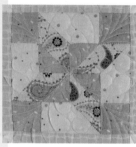

Clay's Choice

Pinwheel Foundation Block

Cutting the Paper Template

Cut four of Template A.

The A appliqués will be cut from the #1 light print rectangle and the #2 medium print rectangle after they are pieced.

Note: *The templates are glued to the wrong side of the fabric. The templates have been reversed for you.*

Piecing

This block consists of 16 pieces.

1 Follow the pinwheel foundation block directions on page 66 to make a pinwheel block. Press all seams open.

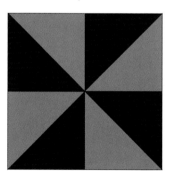

2 Sew the #1 light print rectangle to the #2 medium print rectangle along the 10" side. Press this seam open.

Fabrics

Light Print Fabric:
#1—Cut 1—4" x 10" Rectangle

Medium Print Fabric:
#2—Cut 1—2-1/2" x 10" Rectangle
#3—Cut 1—4-1/2" x 8-1/2" Rectangle

Dark Print Fabric:
#4—Cut 1—4-1/2" x 8-1/2" Rectangle

Refer to General Instructions on pages 10-19 before beginning this block.

3 Glue the A paper templates to the wrong side of the pieced unit, matching the drawn line on the template to the seam line. Trim the fabric 1/4" away from the edge of the templates on all sides.

Note: ✱ on paper templates indicates sides of fabric to be turned.

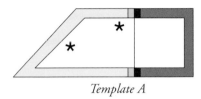

Template A

4 Turn the edges marked with an ✱ on the template.

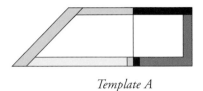

Template A

5 Glue the wrong side of the appliqués in place on the pinwheel block. The raw edges of the appliqué should be placed even with the raw edges of the pinwheel block.

6 Appliqué in place, leaving raw edges open. Follow the directions on pages 18-19 to remove paper templates and glue. Press.

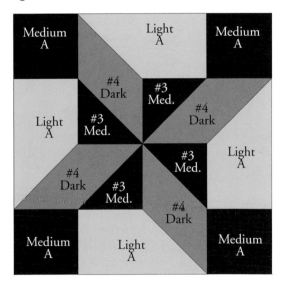

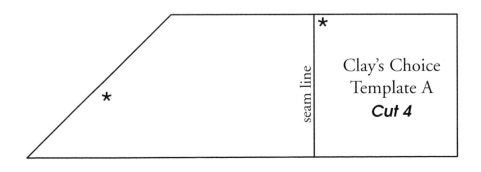

seam line

✱

Clay's Choice
Template A
Cut 4

✱

Shaded Trail

Pinwheel Foundation Block

CUTTING THE PAPER TEMPLATES

Cut four of Templates A and B on page 72.

PIECING

This block consists of 24 pieces.

1 Using Method #1 on page 54, make four half-square triangles from the #1 medium print fabric squares and #4 dark print fabric squares. Press the seams open.

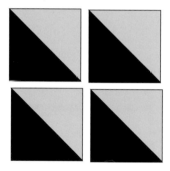

2 Trim the finished half-square triangles to 2-3/4".

3 Follow the pinwheel foundation block directions on page 66 to make a pinwheel from the four half-square triangles. Press all seams open. The pinwheel should measure 5".

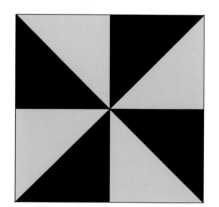

FABRICS

Light Print Fabric:
Scraps to Cut 4 of Appliqué A
& 4 of Appliqué B

Medium Print Fabric:
#1—Cut 2—3-1/2" Squares
#2—Cut 2—1-1/2" x 2-3/4"
Rectangles
#3—Cut 2—1-1/2" x 3-3/4"
Rectangles

Dark Print Fabric:
#4—Cut 2—3-1/2" Squares

#5—Cut 2—1-1/2" x 2-3/4"
Rectangles
#6—Cut 2—1-1/2" x 3-3/4"
Rectangles

*Refer to General Instructions on pages 10-19
before beginning this block.*

4 Sew a #2 medium print fabric rectangle to a #5 dark print fabric rectangle along the 1-1/2" side. Press the seam open. Make a total of two units.

5 Sew these units to opposite sides of the pinwheel, matching the seams. Press the seams open.

6 Sew a #3 medium print fabric rectangle to a #6 dark print fabric rectangle along the 1-1/2" side. Press the seam open. Make a total of two units.

7 Sew these units to the other two sides of the pinwheel, matching the seams. Press the seams open. Trim this pieced block to 6-1/2".

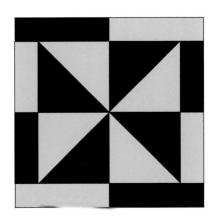

8 Glue the A paper templates to the wrong side of a scrap of light print fabric. Trim the fabric 1/4" away from the templates on all sides. Turn all four sides of the A appliqués.
Note: ✱ on paper templates indicates sides of fabric to be turned.

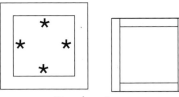

Template A

9 Place the A appliqués on the pieced block, matching the points of the square to the seam lines.

10 Glue the B paper templates to the wrong side of a scrap of light print fabric. Trim the fabric 1/4" away from the templates on all sides. Turn the long side of the B appliqués.

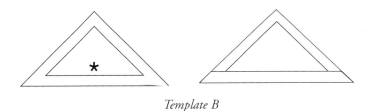

Template B

11 Place the B appliqués on the pieced block. The raw edges of the appliqués should be placed even with the raw edges of the corner of the pieced block.

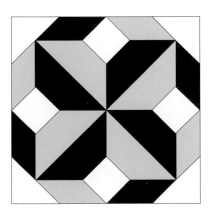

12 Appliqué in place, leaving the raw edges of the B appliqué open. Follow the directions on pages 18-19 to remove paper templates and glue. Press.

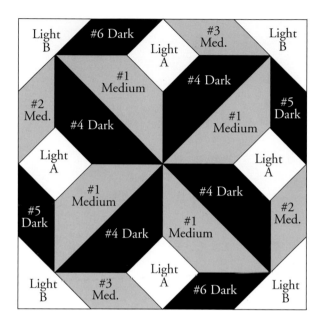

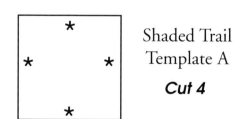

Shaded Trail
Template A

Cut 4

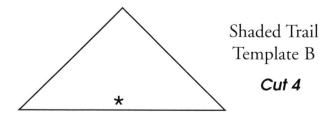

Shaded Trail
Template B

Cut 4

REMOVING PAPER TEMPLATES

When the stitching is done, place the appliquéd block into warm water for at least twenty minutes to dissolve the glue. Remove the appliquéd block from the water, squeeze out the excess water, and roll in an absorbent towel to remove the last of the water. Smooth the block out on the towel and let dry before removing the paper templates.

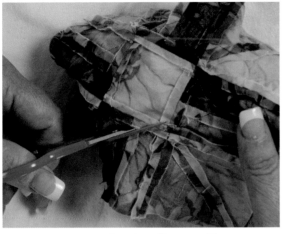

REMOVING THE INSIDE PAPER TEMPLATES

To remove inside templates slit or cut the background fabric. Avoid cutting through the appliquéd stitches.

Remove the inside paper templates. Run the seams under water to remove any remaining glue.

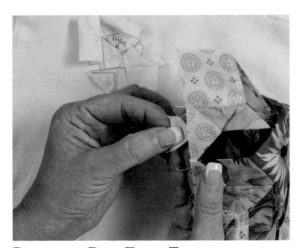

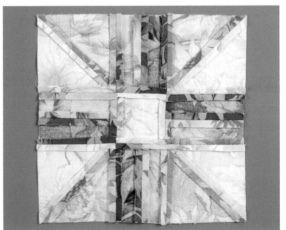

REMOVING RAW EDGE TEMPLATES

Pull out the paper templates along the raw edges of the block. Run the seams under water to flush out any remaining glue. Press the finished appliqué block.

REMOVING EXCESS FABRIC

You may also cut away any excess fabric remaining after removing the paper templates. Be sure to leave the 1/4" seam allowance when trimming the fabric.

LeMoyne Star
Pinwheel Foundation Block

CUTTING THE PAPER TEMPLATES

Cut four of Templates A and B.

> **Note:** *The A & B appliqués are cut out of four of the half-square triangles.*

PIECING

This block consists of 16 pieces.

1 Follow the pinwheel foundation block directions on page 66 to make a pinwheel from four of the half-square triangles. Press all seams open.

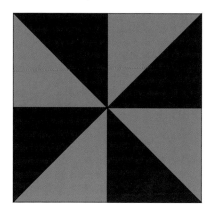

2 Glue the A and B paper templates to the wrong side of the remaining four half-square triangles. Match the drawn line on the templates to the seam lines of the half-square triangles.

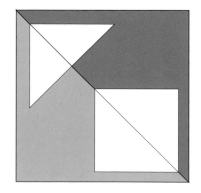

3 Trim the fabric EXACTLY 1/4" away from all sides of the templates. Turn two adjoining sides of alternate colors of the squares. Turn the two short sides of the triangles.

Note: ✳ *on paper templates indicates sides of fabric to be turned.*

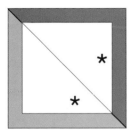
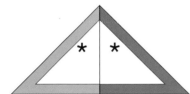

Template A

Template B

4 Glue the wrong side of the A appliqués in place on the pieced pinwheel block. Match the seam lines of the appliqués to the seam lines of the pinwheel foundation block. The raw edge of the appliqués should be placed even with the raw edge of the pinwheel block.

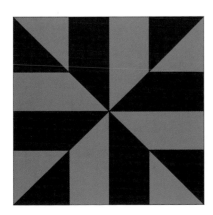

5 Glue the wrong side of the B appliqués in place on the pinwheel block. Match the seam lines of the appliqués to the seam lines of the block. The raw edge of the appliqués should be placed even with the raw edge of the block.

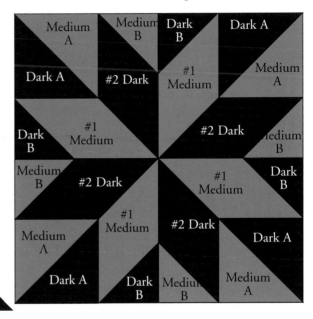

6 Appliqué in place, leaving raw edges open. Follow directions on pages 18-19 to remove the templates and glue. Press.

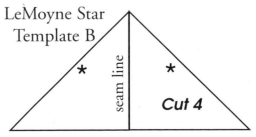

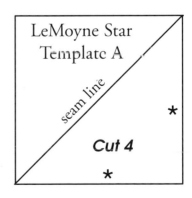

Lone Star

Pinwheel Foundation Block

CUTTING THE PAPER TEMPLATES

Cut four of Templates A, B, and C on page 78.

> **Note:** The A appliqués are cut out of the half-square triangles so the outer edges are on the straight of grain.

> **Note:** If you are going to machine appliqué the block, see instructions on page 15. These instructions are written for hand appliqué.

PIECING

This block consists of 16 pieces.

1 Follow the pinwheel foundation block directions on page 66 to make a pinwheel from four of the half-square triangles. Press all seams open.

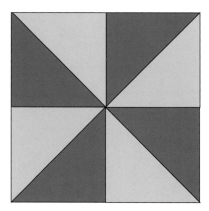

 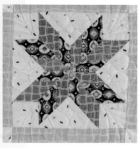

FABRICS

Light Print Fabric:
Scraps to Cut 4 of Appliqué A, 4 of Appliqué B, & 4 of Appliqué C

Medium Print Fabric:
#1—Cut 1—9" Square

Dark Print Fabric:
#2—Cut 1—9" Square

Refer to General Instructions on pages 10-19 before beginning this block.

2 Glue the A paper templates to the wrong side of the four remaining half-square triangles. Match the drawn line on the template to the seam line on the half-square triangles. Trim the fabric EXACTLY 1/4" away from all sides of the templates. Turn two adjoining sides of alternate colors.

> **Note:** ★ on paper templates indicates sides of fabric to be turned.

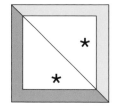

Template A

3 Place the A appliqués on the pinwheel block, alternating colors.

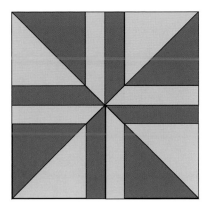

4 Glue the B paper templates to the wrong side of a scrap of light print fabric. Trim the fabric 1/4" away from all sides of the templates. Turn two adjoining sides of the B appliqués.

Template B

5 Glue the wrong side of the B appliqués in place on the pieced pinwheel block. The raw edges of the appliqués should be placed even with the raw edges of the pinwheel block.

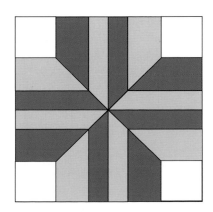

6 Glue the C paper templates to the wrong side of a scrap of light print fabric. Trim the fabric EXACTLY 1/4" away from all sides of the templates. Turn the two short sides of the C appliqués.

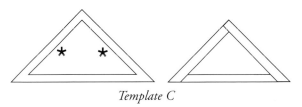

Template C

7 Glue the wrong side of the C appliqués in place on the pieced pinwheel block. The raw edge of the appliqués should be placed even with the raw edge of the pinwheel block.

8 Appliqué in place, leaving raw edges open. Follow directions on pages 18-19 to remove templates and glue. Press.

Lone Star continued

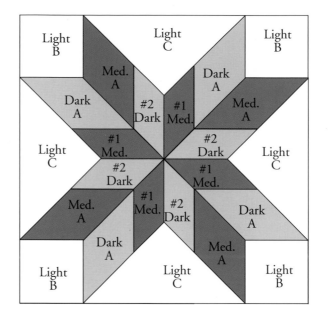

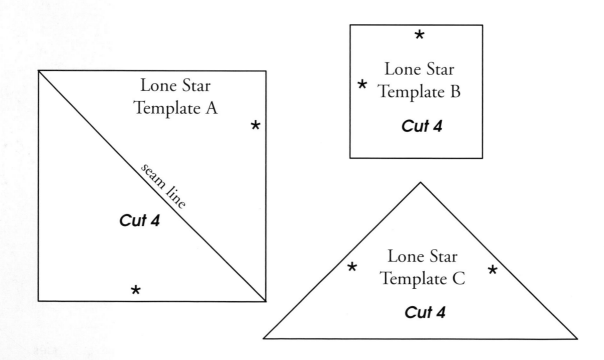

Lone Star
Template A

seam line

Cut 4

*

*

Lone Star
Template B

Cut 4

*

*

Lone Star
Template C

Cut 4

*

*

MAKE THE FOUNDATION BLOCK

Half-square triangles are used to make the pinwheel foundation block shown above. Four additional half-square triangles are used to create the A appliqués in the Lone Star block.

PLACE THE PIECED APPLIQUÉS

Place the seam of the turned A appliqués, made from the pieced half-square triangles, on the seam of the pinwheel foundation block. The raw edges of the appliqués should be placed even with the raw edges of the foundation block.

GLUE THE APPLIQUÉS TO THE BLOCK

Glue the B and C appliqués in place on the block. The point of the triangle and one corner of the square should line up with the block's seam line. The raw edges of the appliqués should align with the raw edges of the block.

FINISH THE BLOCK

Use a 6-1/2" ruler to trim the appliqués even with the foundation block. Stitch the appliqués in place, leaving raw edges open. Follow directions on pages 18-19 to remove paper templates and glue. Press.

E-Z Quilt

Pinwheel Foundation Block

CUTTING THE PAPER TEMPLATES

Cut four of Templates A and B on page 83.
Cut one of Templates C and D on page 83. The
fabric for the D appliqué is cut from a pieced unit.

PIECING

This block consists of 20 pieces.

> **Note:** If you are going to machine appliqué
> the block, see instructions on page 15. These
> instructions are written for hand appliqué.

1 Follow the pinwheel foundation block
directions on page 66 to make a pinwheel
from the four half-square triangles. Press all
seams open.

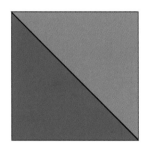

Make 4

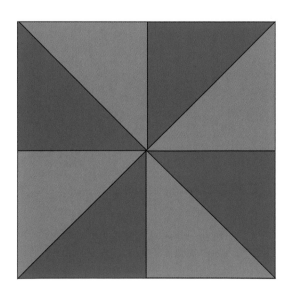

FABRICS

Light Print Fabric:
Scraps to Cut 4 of Appliqué A
& 4 of Appliqué B
#1—Cut 1—1" Square

Medium Light Print Fabric:
#2—Cut 2—1" x 3-1/4" Rectangles
Scraps to Cut 1 of Appliqué C

Medium Print Fabric:
#3—Cut 1—4-1/2" x 8-1/2"
Rectangle

Medium Dark Print Fabric:
#4—Cut 1—4-1/2" x 8-1/2"
Rectangle

*Refer to General Instructions on pages 10-19
before beginning this block.*

2 Glue the A paper templates to the wrong side of a scrap of light print fabric. Trim the fabric EXACTLY 1/4" away from templates on all sides. Turn the two short sides of the A appliqués. **Note:** ⋆ *on paper templates indicates sides of fabric to be turned.*

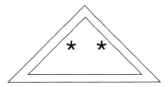

Template A

3 Glue the wrong side of the appliqués in place on the pieced pinwheel block. The raw edge of the appliqués should be placed even with the raw edge of the pinwheel.

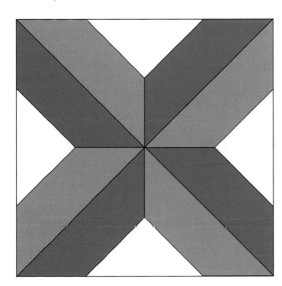

4 Glue the B paper templates to the wrong side of a scrap of light print fabric. Trim the fabric EXACTLY 1/4" away from templates on all sides. Turn two adjoining sides of the B appliqués.

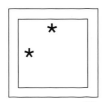

Template B

5 Glue the wrong side of the appliqués in place on the pieced pinwheel block. The raw edge of the appliqués should be placed even with the raw edge of the pinwheel.

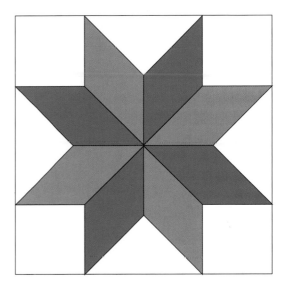

6 Glue the C paper template to the wrong side of a scrap of medium light print fabric. Trim the fabric EXACTLY 1/4" away from the template on all sides. Turn the two long sides of the appliqué.

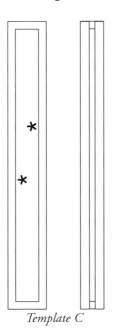

Template C

7 Center and glue the C appliqué on the pinwheel foundation block.

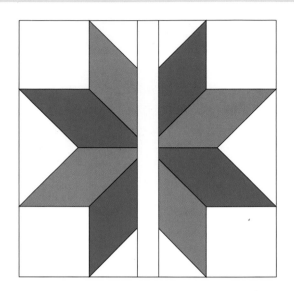

8 Sew a #2 medium light print rectangle to opposite sides of the #1 light print square. Press the seams open.

9 Glue the D paper template to the wrong side of the unit pieced in Step #8 matching the drawn lines on the template to the seam lines of the pieced unit. Turn the two long edges of the appliqué.

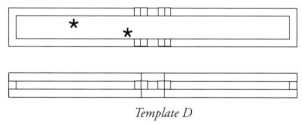

Template D

10 Center and glue the D appliqué on the block in Step #9. Place the D appliqué over the C appliqué so that the center square crosses it.

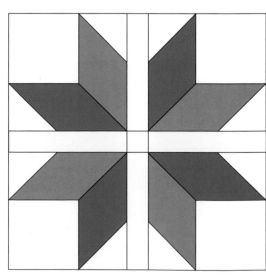

11 Appliqué in place, leaving raw edges open. Follow directions on pages 18-19 to remove paper templates and glue. Press.

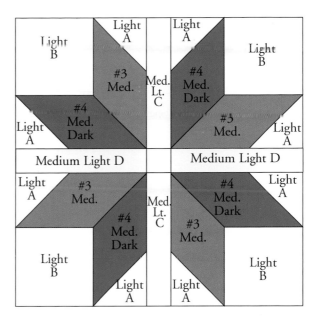

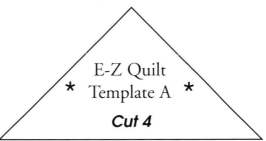

E-Z Quilt
Template A

* *

Cut 4

*
E-Z Quilt
Template B
*

Cut 4

Cut 1
*
*
E-Z Quilt Template C

E-Z Quilt Template D | *Cut 1*
*
*

Kaleidoscope Foundation Block

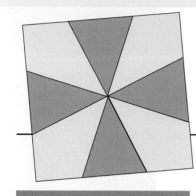

A Kaleidoscope Block is cut from a pinwheel block.

Make a sample block to learn the technique before cutting the fabric for your quilt.

FABRICS

Cut 2—6" Squares from Light Fabric

Cut 2—6" Squares from Dark Fabric

PIECING

1 Using Method #1 on page 54, make four half-square triangles from the 6" squares of light and dark fabrics. Trim these finished half-square triangles to 5".

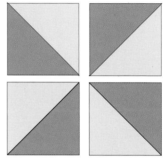

2 Sew four half-square triangles together to form a pinwheel. Press the seams open.

CUTTING THE KALEIDOSCOPE:

3 Glue the kaleidoscope template to the wrong side of the pinwheel block, matching the lines on the template to the seam lines of the pinwheel. The kaleidoscope block instructions state which fabric should be on the corners. Place the template accordingly.

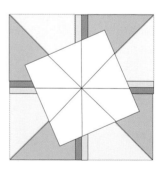

4 Place the 6-1/2" Creative Grids™ *Square It Up & Fussy Cut* ruler on top of the template so that the 1/4" seam extends beyond the template on all sides.

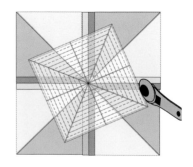

5 Cut around the ruler on all sides.

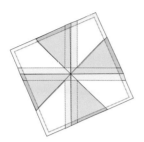

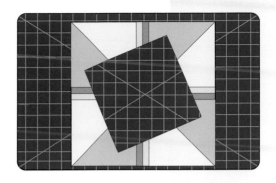

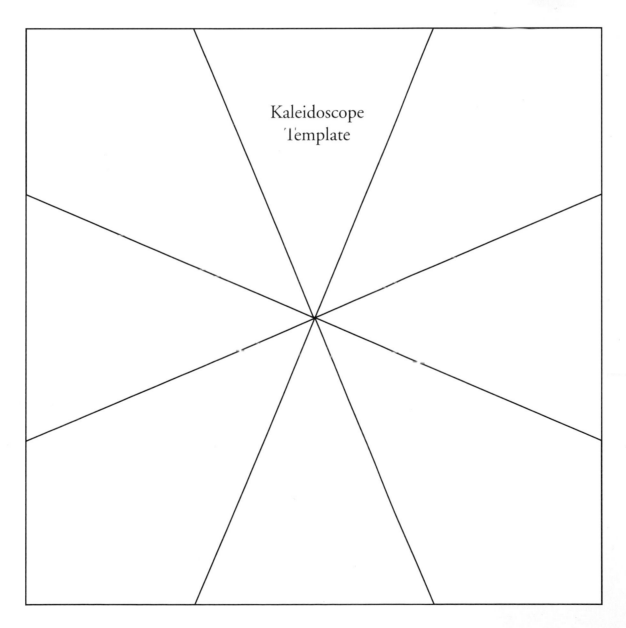

Kaleidoscope
Template

Purple Cross

Kaleidoscope Foundation Block

CUTTING THE PAPER TEMPLATES

Cut four of Templates A and B on page 88.
Cut one of Template C on page 89.

PIECING

This block consists of 17 pieces.

> **Note:** *The templates are glued to the wrong side of the fabric. Therefore, the turned appliqué is a mirror image of the original template. In this case, the A & B templates are mirror images of each other. The templates provided have been reversed for you.*
> *The C template is reverse appliquéd. Therefore, you must cut out the center circle. Because this appliqué touches the finished edge of the block on all four sides, this template includes the seam allowance.*

1 Following the kaleidoscope foundation block directions on page 84, make a kaleidoscope block with the #1 medium print fabric squares and the #2 medium dark print fabric squares. Trim the kaleidoscope so that the medium dark print fabric will form the corners of the block.

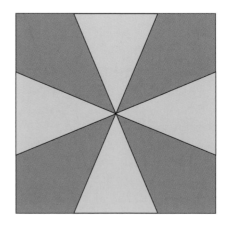

> **Note:** *If you are going to machine appliqué the block, see instructions on page 15. These instructions are written for hand appliqué.*

FABRICS

Light Print Fabric:
Scraps to Cut 4 of Appliqué A & B

Medium Print Fabric:
#1—Cut 2—6" Squares

Medium Dark Print Fabric:
#2—Cut 2—6" Squares

Dark Print Fabric:
Scrap to Cut 1 of Appliqué C

*Refer to General Instructions on pages 10-19
before beginning this block.*

2 Glue the A paper templates to the wrong side of a scrap of light print fabric. Trim the fabric EXACTLY 1/4" away from all sides of the templates. Turn the edges marked with an * on the template. Glue the wrong side of the appliqués in place on the kaleidoscope foundation block. The raw edges of the appliqués should be placed even with the raw edges of the kaleidoscope foundation block.

Note: ✸ *on paper templates indicates sides of fabric to be turned.*

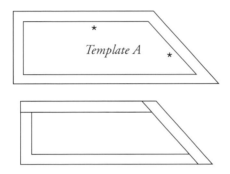

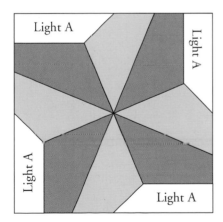

3 Glue the B paper template to the wrong side of a scrap of light print fabric. Trim the fabric EXACTLY 1/4" away from all sides of the templates. Glue the wrong side of the appliqués in place on the kaleidoscope foundation block.

The raw edges of the appliqués should be placed even with the raw edges of the kaleidoscope foundation block.

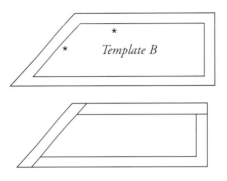

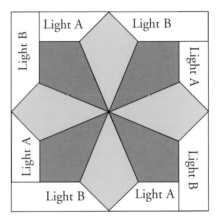

4 Glue the C paper template to the wrong side of the scrap of dark print fabric. The C template includes the outer seam allowance. Therefore, cut the fabric even with the outer edge of the template and do not turn this edge. Trim the fabric 1/4" away from the inner circle of the template. Clip and turn the inner edge.

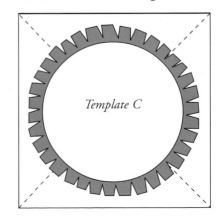

Purple Cross continued

5 Glue the wrong side of the C appliqué to the kaleidoscope block.

6 Appliqué in place, leaving raw edges open. Follow directions on pages 18-19 to remove paper templates and glue. Press.

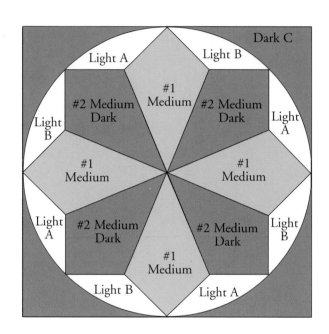

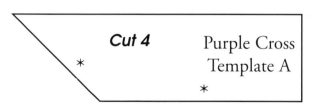

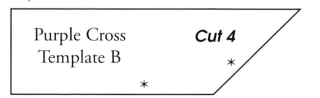

Purple Cross Template C

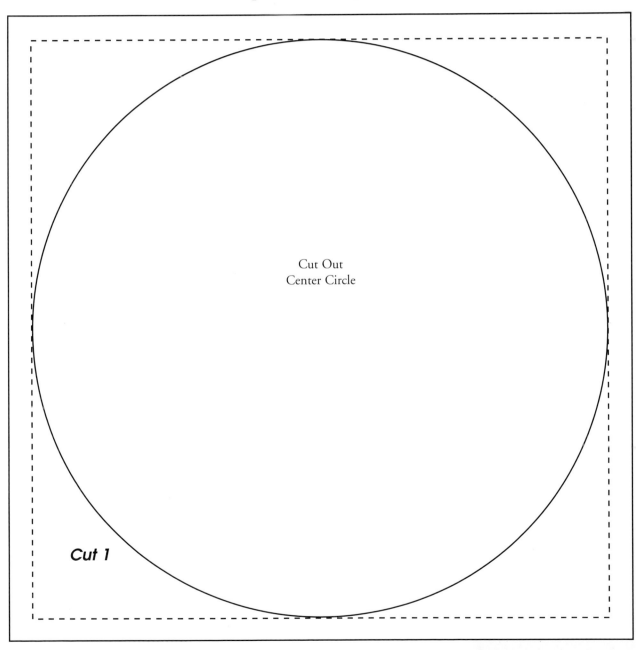

Cut Out
Center Circle

Cut 1

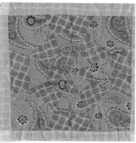

Spider Web

Kaleidoscope Foundation Block

CUTTING THE PAPER TEMPLATES

Cut one of Templates A and B on page 92. The A and B appliqués are cut from pieced kaleidoscope blocks.

> **Note:** *Even though the kaleidoscopes in the completed block are three different sizes, the cutting instructions are the same. The center of ONE kaleidoscope shows. By making them all the same size, you can choose the one with the "perfect center" for appliqué B. If your centers ALWAYS match, you can make two kaleidoscopes and cut the B appliqué from the center of the foundation block **after** the A appliqué is stitched. If you choose to do this cut 4—6" squares of each print. Refer to Technique Notebook on page 93.*
>
> **Note:** *If you are going to machine appliqué the block, see instructions on page 15. These instructions are written for hand appliqué.*

PIECING

This block consists of 24 pieces.

1. Following the kaleidoscope foundation block directions on page 84, make three kaleidoscope blocks with the #1 medium print fabric squares and the #2 dark print fabric squares. The medium print fabric should form the corners of the blocks. One of these blocks will be your foundation block.

 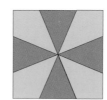 

FABRICS

Medium Print Fabric:
#1—Cut 6—6" Squares
Dark Print Fabric:
#2—Cut 6—6" Squares

Refer to General Instructions on pages 10-19 before beginning this block.

2 Glue the A and B paper templates to the wrong side of two of the kaleidoscope blocks. Trim the fabric EXACTLY 1/4" away from all sides of the templates. Turn all sides.

Note: ★ *on paper templates indicates sides of fabric to be turned.*

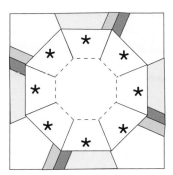

Template A

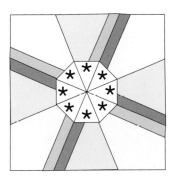

Template B

3 Center and glue the wrong side of appliqué A in place on the kaleidoscope foundation block. Place the medium print fabrics of the appliqué on the dark print fabrics of the kaleidoscope.

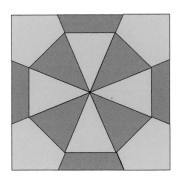

4 Center and glue the wrong side of appliqué B in place on appliqué A. Place the medium print fabrics of appliqué B on the dark print fabrics of appliqué A.

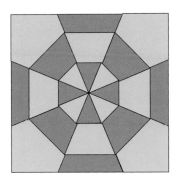

5 Appliqué in place. Follow directions on pages 18-19 to remove paper templates and glue. Press.

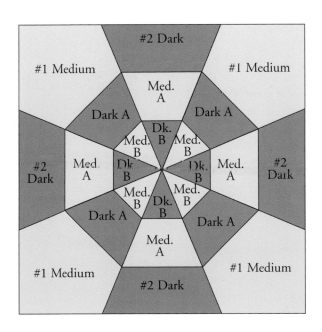

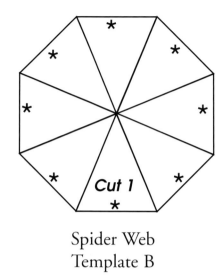

Spider Web
Template B

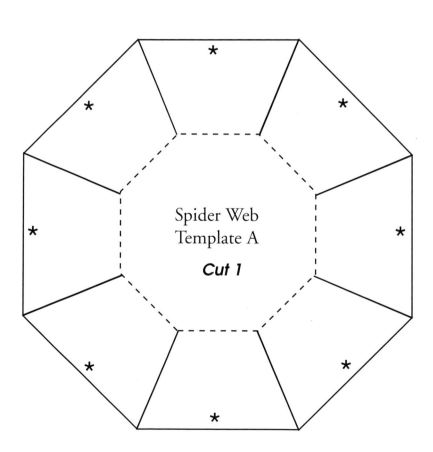

Spider Web
Template A

Cut 1

CUT TEMPLATE FROM KALEIDOSCOPE BLOCK

Glue the A paper template to the wrong side of one of the two kaleidoscope blocks. Trim the fabric EXACTLY 1/4" away from all sides of the template. Pull out a few stitches and turn in all the light sides of the appliqués, then all the dark sides.

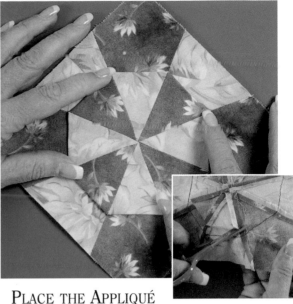

PLACE THE APPLIQUÉ

Center and glue the wrong side of appliqué A in place on the kaleidoscope foundation block. Appliqué in place. *As shown in inset photo,* carefully cut the background fabric with a 1/4" seam allowance. Avoid cutting through the appliquéd stitches.

GLUE PAPER TEMPLATE B

Using the fabric you cut away from the kaleidoscope foundation block, glue paper template B to the wrong side of the fabric. Trim the fabric EXACTLY 1/4" away from all sides of the template. Turn all sides. *We did not remove paper template A from the foundation block to show where the fabric used for template B was cut away. You will want to remove the paper template before gluing appliqué B to the foundation block.*

FINISH THE SPIDER WEB BLOCK

Center and glue the wrong side of appliqué B in place on appliqué A. Stitch in place. Follow directions on pages 18-19 to remove paper templates and glue. Press.

Quarter-Square Triangle Foundation Block

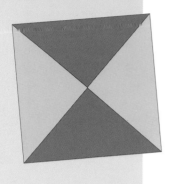

A quarter-square triangle block consists of four equal sized triangles. It is sewn from two half-square triangles.

Note: Generally, when making quarter-square triangle blocks, the squares should be cut 1-1/4" larger than the finished block. In some cases, they are cut even larger so appliqués can be cut from the pieced quarter-square triangle foundation block. Since you are sewing bias edges, the sewing and pressing tend to distort the shape of your finished square. I add 2" so I can square up the quarter-square triangles to the correct size after stitching and pressing.

Make a sample block to learn the technique before cutting the fabric for your quilt.

FABRICS

Cut 1—8" Square of a Light Fabric

Cut 1—8" Square of a Dark Fabric

Note: *Fabric sizes given are for a quarter-square triangle sample block. Refer to your chosen block for specific fabric requirements.*

PIECING

1 Make two half-square triangles with the 8" squares of light fabric and dark fabric. Press the seams open.

2 Place one half-square triangle on top of the other half-square triangle, right sides together, matching seams. The light triangle should be placed on the dark triangle.

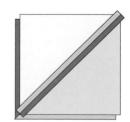

3 Draw a diagonal line on the wrong side of the half-square triangle units. You will cross the seam line. Sew a 1/4" seam on each side of the drawn line. Fold the top half-square triangle back 1/4" away from the drawn line and match the seam lines. Put a dab of glue in place so your points will match perfectly.

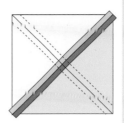

4 Cut on the drawn line. Press this final seam open. You have created two quarter-square triangles.

5 Place the Creative Grids™ *Square It Up & Fussy Cut* ruler on top of the finished quarter-square triangle block, matching the diagonal lines on the ruler to the seam lines of the block. Cut around the ruler on all sides to trim the finished block to 6-1/2".

Note: In some cases, one quarter-square triangle will be used as the foundation block and will be trimmed to 6-1/2". Appliqués will be cut from the other quarter-square triangle so it should not be trimmed.

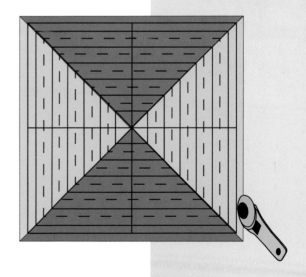

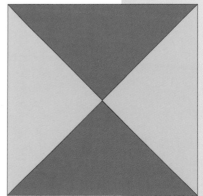

Jewel Star

Quarter-Square Triangle Foundation Block

CUTTING THE PAPER TEMPLATES

Cut four of Templates A and B on page 98.

> **Note:** *The fabric for the A appliqués will be cut from one of the quarter-square triangle blocks. By placing and cutting the A templates from a pieced quarter-square triangle block, the raw edge of the appliqué is on the straight of the grain of the fabric so the finished block is more stable.*
>
> **Note:** *If you are going to machine appliqué the block, see instructions on page 15. These instructions are written for hand appliqué.*

PIECING

This block consists of 16 pieces.

1 Following the quarter-square triangle foundation block directions on page 94, make two quarter-square triangles with the #1 medium print fabric square and the #2 dark print fabric square.

2 Choose the block that has the best center seam match for the foundation block. Trim this block to 6 -1/2". Do not trim the other quarter-square triangle block.

FABRICS

Light Print Fabric:
Scraps to Cut 4 of Appliqué B

Medium Print Fabric:
#1—Cut 1—11" Square

Dark Print Fabric:
#2—Cut 1—11" Square

Refer to General Instructions on pages 10-19 before beginning this block.

3 Place and glue the A paper templates to the wrong side of the remaining quarter square triangle foundation block—at least 1/4" away from the outside edge. Match the drawn lines on the templates to the seam lines of the quarter-square triangle. Trim the fabric 1/4" away from the templates on all sides. Pull out a few stitches and turn the two short sides of each appliqué. Do not turn the other side.

Note: ✳ *on paper templates indicates sides of fabric to be turned.*

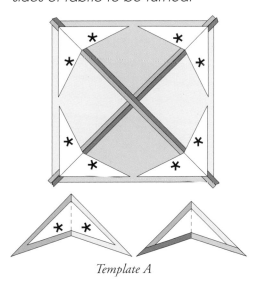

Template A

4 Glue the wrong side of the A appliqués in place on the trimmed quarter-square triangle block. The points of the appliqués will overlap. The raw edges of the appliqués should be placed even with the raw edges of the quarter-square triangle block.

5 Glue the B paper templates to the wrong side of a scrap of light print fabric. Trim the fabric 1/4" away from the templates on all sides. Turn the two short sides of the B templates. Do not turn the other side.

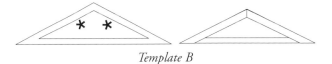

Template B

6 Place and glue the wrong side of the B appliqués in place over the A appliqués.

7 Appliqué in place, leaving raw edges open. Follow directions on pages 18-19 to remove paper templates and glue. Press.

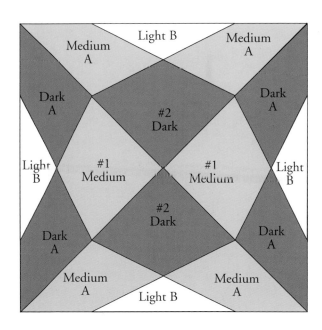

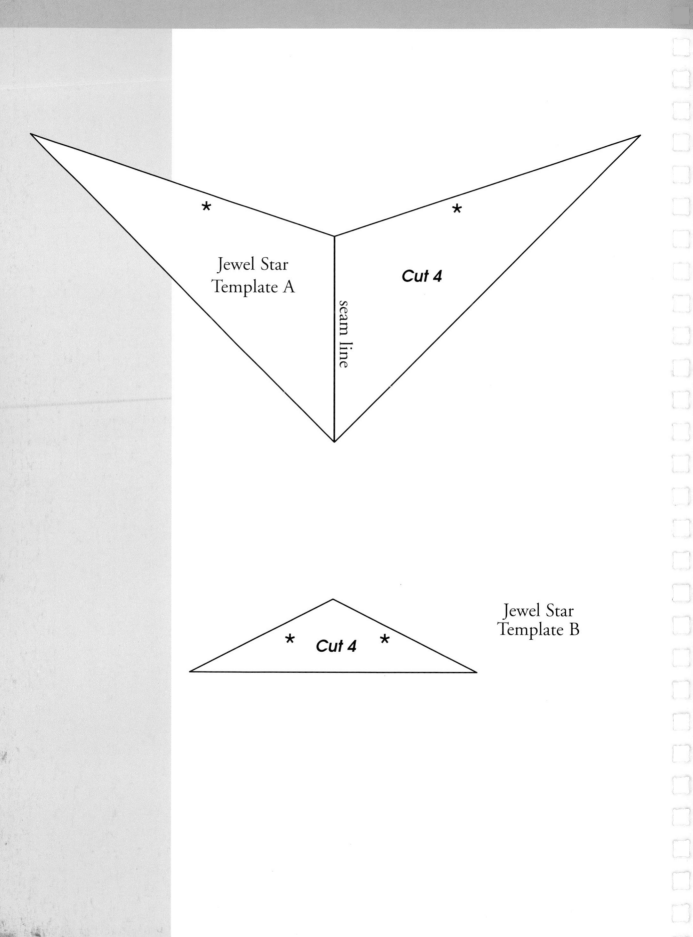

Jewel Star
Template A

*

Cut 4

*

seam line

* Cut 4 *

Jewel Star
Template B

TRIM THE FOUNDATION BLOCK

Trim one of the finished quarter-square triangle blocks to 6-1/2". This will be the foundation block. The second quarter-square triangle block should NOT be trimmed.

GLUE THE PAPER TEMPLATES

Glue the A paper templates to the wrong side of the remaining quarter-square triangle block. Match the drawn line on the template to the seam lines of the quarter-square triangle.

PLACE THE APPLIQUÉS

Glue the wrong side of the A appliqués in place on the trimmed quarter-square triangle block. The points of the appliqués will overlap. The raw edges of the appliqués should be placed even with the raw edges of the corners of the quarter-square triangle.

FINISH THE PIECED APPLIQUÉ™ BLOCK

Glue the wrong side of the B appliqués in place over the A appliqués. Stitch the layered appliqués in place, leaving the raw edges open. Remove paper templates and glue, referring to pages 18-19.

Spools

Quarter-Square Triangle Foundation Block

CUTTING THE PAPER TEMPLATE

Cut four of Template A.

PIECING

This block consists of 20 pieces.

1 Following the quarter-square triangle block directions on page 94, make four quarter-square triangles with the #1 medium print fabric squares and the #2 dark print fabric squares.

2 **Trim these quarter-square triangles to 3-1/2".**

3 Sew the four quarter-square triangles together to form the foundation block.

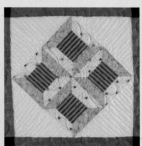
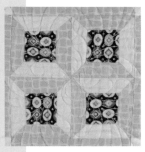

FABRICS

Light Print Fabric:
Scraps to Cut 4 of Appliqué A

Medium Print Fabric:
#1—Cut 2—4-1/2" Squares

Dark Print Fabric:
#2—Cut 2—4-1/2" Squares

Refer to General Instructions on pages 10-19 before beginning this block.

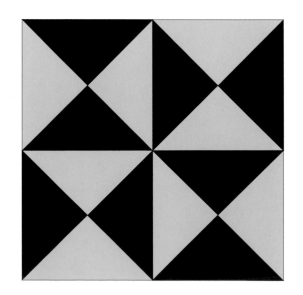

4 Glue the A paper templates to the wrong side of a scrap of light print fabric. Trim the fabric 1/4" away from the templates on all sides. Turn all sides. **Note:** ★ on paper templates indicates sides of fabric to be turned.

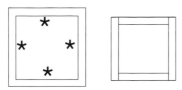

Template A

5 Place and glue the wrong side of the A appliqués in place on the foundation block. The points of the A appliqués should touch the seam lines of each quarter-square triangle.

6 Appliqué in place. Follow directions on pages 18-19 to remove paper templates and glue. Press.

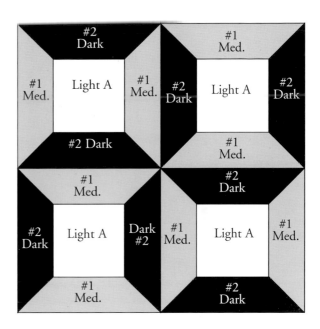

★
Spools
★ Template A ★
Cut 4
★

Set on Point Foundation Block

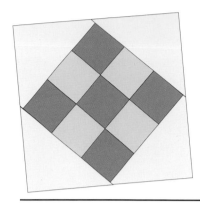

When a block or quilt is set on point, it is turned 90 degrees. In the Saw Tooth block on page 106, a nine-patch is placed on point by sewing triangles to opposite sides of the center square.

Make a sample block to learn the technique before cutting the fabric for your quilt.

FABRICS

Light Print: #1
Cut 2—4-1/2" Squares

Cut once on the Diagonal

Medium Print: #2
Cut 4—1-7/8" Squares

Dark Print: #3
Cut 5—1-7/8" Squares

PIECING

1 Following the nine-patch block directions on page 44, make a nine-patch from the #2 medium print squares and the #3 dark print squares. Press all seams open.

2 Center and sew a light print triangle to opposite sides of the nine-patch. Press the seams open.

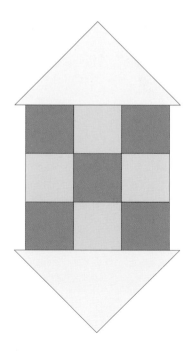

3 Trim off the points of the triangle even with the sides of the nine-patch.

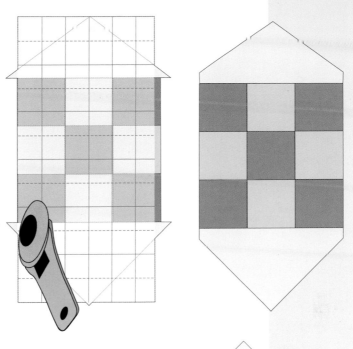

4 Center and sew a light print triangle to the remaining two sides of the nine-patch. Press the seams open.

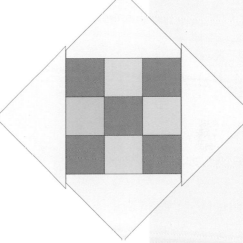

5 Place the Creative Grids™ *Square It Up & Fussy Cut* ruler on the block so that the horizontal and vertical lines on the ruler intersect the points of the nine-patch. If your seam allowances are accurate, the seam allowance should extend 1/4" away from the corners of the nine-patch.

6 Trim all four sides.

Baton Rouge

Set on Point Foundation Block

Cutting the Paper Templates

Cut one of Template A and four of Template B.

> **Note:** *Fussy cutting these appliqués can have a dramatic effect on the finished block.*

Piecing

This block consists of 25 pieces.

1 Following the quarter-square block directions on page 94, make four quarter-square triangles with the #2 medium print squares and the #3 dark print squares. Press the seams open.

2 **Trim the finished quarter-square triangles to 3-3/8".**

3 Sew these quarter-square triangles together, alternating colors. Press the seams open.

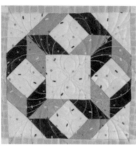

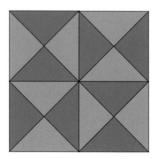

4 Follow the Set on Point Foundation directions on page 102 to set the pieced quarter-square triangles on point using the #1 light print fabric triangles.

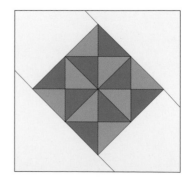

Fabrics

Light Print Fabric:
#1—Cut 2—6-1/2" Squares
Cut once on the Diagonal
Scraps to Cut 4 of Appliqué B

Medium Light Print Fabric:
Scraps to Cut 1 of Appliqué A

Medium Print Fabric:
#2—Cut 2—4-1/2" Squares

Dark Print Fabric:
#3—Cut 2—4-1/2" Squares

Refer to General Instructions on pages 10-19 before beginning this block.

5 Glue the A paper template to the wrong side of a scrap of medium light print fabric. Trim the fabric EXACTLY 1/4" away from the template on all sides. Turn all sides.

Note: ✷ on paper templates indicates sides of fabric to be turned.

Template A

6 Glue the wrong side of the appliqué in place on the pieced block.

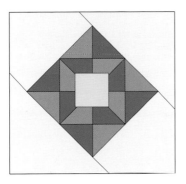

7 Glue the B paper templates to the wrong side of a scrap of light print fabric. Trim the fabric EXACTLY 1/4" away from the templates on all sides. Turn all sides.

Template B

Baton Rouge
Template A

Cut 1

Baton Rouge
Template B

Cut 4

8 Glue the wrong side of the appliqués in place on the pieced block.

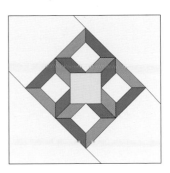

9 **Trim this pieced block to 6-1/2" - 1/4" beyond the points of the B appliqués.**

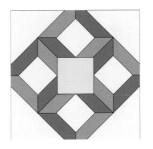

10 Appliqué in place. Follow directions on pages 18-19 to remove paper templates and glue. Press.

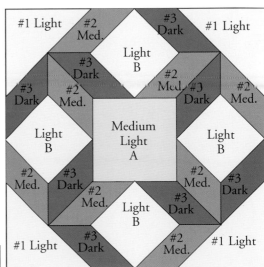

105

Saw Tooth

Set on Point Foundation Block

CUTTING THE PAPER TEMPLATE

Cut four of Template A.
The A appliqués are cut from
four half-square triangles.

PIECING

This block consists of 21 pieces.

1 Following the nine-patch foundation block directions on page 44, make a nine-patch with the #3 medium print squares and the #4 dark print squares. Press all seams open.

2 Follow the Set on Point Foundation directions on page 102 to set the pieced nine-patch on point using the #2 light print fabric triangles.

3 Trim this pieced block to 6-1/2" - 3-1/4" from the center point.

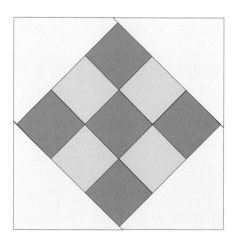

FABRICS

Light Print Fabric:
#1—Cut 2—3-1/2" Squares
#2—Cut 2—4-1/2" Squares
Cut once on the Diagonal

Medium Print Fabric:
#3—Cut 4—1-7/8" Squares
Dark Print Fabric:
#4—Cut 5—1-7/8" Squares
#5—Cut 2—3-1/2" Squares

*Refer to General Instructions on pages 10-19
before beginning this block.*

4 Using Method #1 on page 54, make four half-square triangles with the #1 light print squares and the #5 dark print squares. Press the seams open.

5 Glue the A paper templates to the wrong side of the half-square triangles, matching the drawn line on the template to the seam line of the half-square triangle. Trim the fabric EXACTLY 1/4" away from all sides of the templates. Turn the two adjoining dark sides of the A appliqués.
Note: ✷ *on paper templates indicates sides of fabric to be turned.*

6 Glue the wrong side of the appliqués in place on the pieced block. The raw edges of the appliqués should be placed even with the raw edges of the pieced block.

7 Appliqué in place, leaving raw edges open. Follow directions on pages 18-19 to remove paper templates and glue. Press.

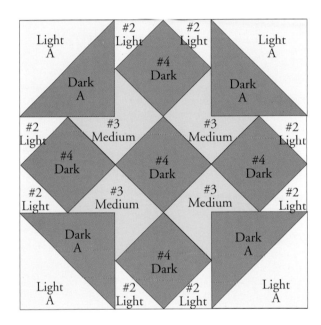

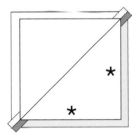

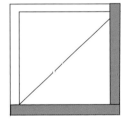

Template A

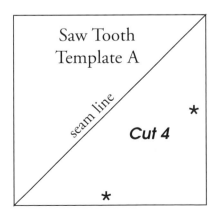

Bright Hopes Foundation Block

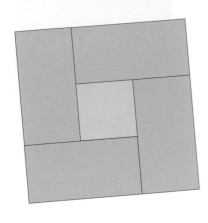

A Bright Hopes block consists of a center square surrounded by four rectangles of equal size. This method eliminates the need to sew an inset point.

Make a sample block to learn the technique before cutting the fabric for your quilt.

PIECING

1 Lay the center square on one of the rectangles, right sides together. Sew a partial seam approximately 1-3/4" long. Press the seam open.

2 Place the seamed edge on a 2-1/2" x 4-1/2" rectangle of fabric, right sides together. Sew along the 4-1/2" length. Press the seam open.

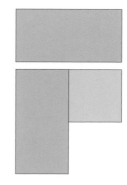

3 Place the seamed edge on a 2-1/2" x 4-1/2" rectangle of fabric, right sides together. Sew along the 4-1/2" length. Press the seam open.

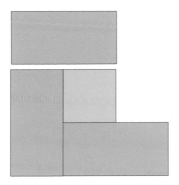

4 Place the seamed edge on a 2-1/2" x 4-1/2" rectangle of fabric, right sides together. Sew along the 4-1/2" length. Press the seam open.

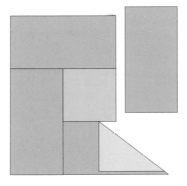

5 Finish sewing the partial seam to connect the first 2-1/2" x 4-1/2" rectangle. Press the seam open.

Rosemary's Star

Bright Hopes Foundation Block

CUTTING THE PAPER TEMPLATES

Cut four of Templates A and B.

PIECING

This block consists of 17 pieces.

1 Following the Bright Hopes foundation block instructions on page 108, piece a Bright Hopes block from the #1 medium print square and the #2 medium dark print rectangles. Press the seams toward the medium dark print rectangles.

2 Follow the Set on Point Foundation directions on page 102 to set the pieced Bright Hopes block on point using the #3 dark print fabric triangles.

3 Trim the pieced block to 6-1/2" – 3-1/4" from the center point.

FABRICS

Light Print Fabric:
Scraps to Cut 4 of Appliqués A & B

Medium Print Fabric:
#1—Cut 1—2" Square

Medium Dark Print Fabric:
#2—Cut 4—1-1/8" x 2-5/8"
Rectangles

Dark Print Fabric:
#3—Cut 2—5-1/4" Squares
Cut Once on the Diagonal

Refer to General Instructions on pages 10-19 before beginning this block.

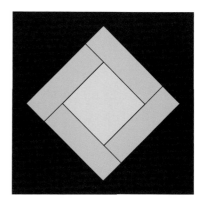

4 Glue the A paper templates to the wrong side of a scrap of light print fabric. Trim the fabric 1/4" away from the templates on all sides. Turn two adjoining sides.

Note: ★ on paper templates indicates sides of fabric to be turned.

Template A

5 Glue the wrong side of the A appliqués in place on the pieced Bright Hopes block.

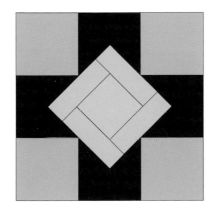

6 Glue the B paper templates to the wrong side of a scrap of light print fabric. Trim the fabric 1/4" away from the templates on all sides. Turn the two short sides .

Template B

7 Glue the wrong side of the B appliqués in place on the pieced Bright Hopes block.

8 Appliqué in place, leaving raw edges open. Follow directions on pages 18-19 to remove paper templates and glue. Press.

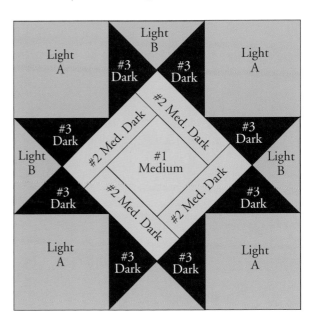

Rosemary's Star
Template A

Cut 4

Cut 4

Rosemary's Star
Template B

Bright Hopes Foundation Block

CUTTING THE PAPER TEMPLATE

Cut four of Template A.

PIECING

This block consists of 16 pieces.

1 Following the quarter-square foundation block directions on page 94, make two quarter-square triangles with the #1 light print fabric and the #3 light medium print fabric. You need one, so choose the block that has the best center seam match. Trim to 3".

2 Glue the wrong side of the A paper templates to a scrap of dark print fabric. Trim the fabric EXACTLY 1/4" away from the template on all sides. Turn the longest side. Refer to the Technique Notebook on page 114.

Note: ★ *on paper templates indicates sides of fabric to be turned.*

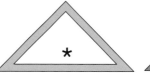

Template A

3 Glue these appliqués to the #4 medium print rectangles.

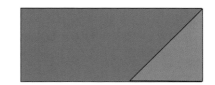

FABRICS

Light Print Fabric:
#1—Cut 1—4" Square
#2—Cut 2—5" Squares
Cut Once on the Diagonal

Light Medium Print Fabric:
#3—Cut 1—4" Square

Medium Print Fabric:
#4—Cut 4—2-1/4" x 4-3/4"
Rectangles

Dark Print Fabric:
Scraps to Cut 4 of Appliqué A

Refer to General Instructions on pages 10-19 before beginning this block.

4 Appliqué in place. Follow directions on pages 18-19 to remove paper templates and glue. Press.

5 Following the Bright Hopes foundation block instructions on page 108, piece a Bright Hopes block from the pieced quarter-square triangle and the #4 appliquéd medium print rectangles. Press the seams toward the medium print rectangles.

6 Follow the Set on Point Foundation directions on page 102 to set the pieced Bright Hopes block on point using the #2 light print fabric triangles.

7 **Trim the finished block to 6-1/2" – 1/4" beyond the points of the A appliqués.**

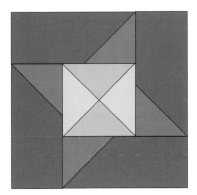

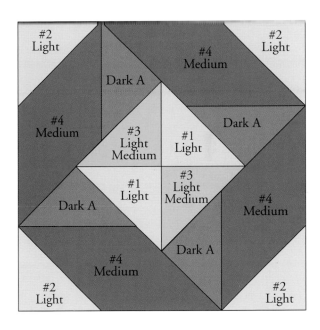

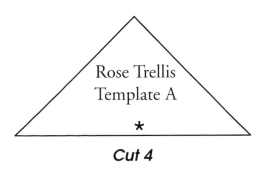

Rose Trellis
Template A

*

Cut 4

Turn the Appliqués

Glue the paper template to the wrong side of your fabric. Turn the longest side of the triangle appliqué.

Place the Appliqués

Glue the appliqués to the rectangles aligning the raw edges of the appliqués with the raw edges of the fabric rectangle. Appliqué in place. Follow the directions on pages 18-19 to remove the paper templates and glue. These pieces will be used to construct the Rose Trellis Bright Hopes foundation block.

Make the Foundation Block

Piece a Bright Hopes foundation block, following instructions on page 108, from the quarter-square triangle and the appliquéd rectangles. Press the seams toward the rectangles.

Sew the Triangle Units

Center and sew a triangle unit to one side of the Bright Hopes foundation block. The unit is over-sized.

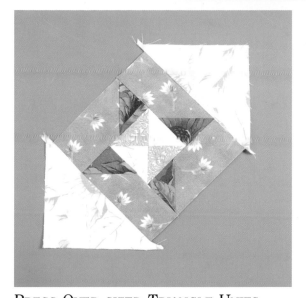

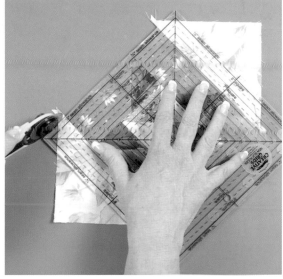

PRESS OVER-SIZED TRIANGLE UNITS

Center and sew a second triangle unit to the opposite side of the Bright Hopes foundation block. Press the seams toward the triangles.

TRIM THE TRIANGLE POINTS

Trim the points of the over-sized triangle units even with the Bright Hopes block.

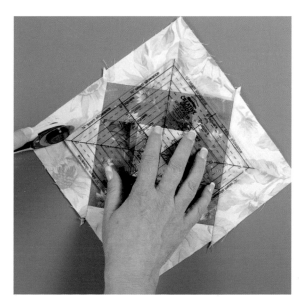

TRIM THE PIECED APPLIQUÉ BLOCK

Sew the two remaining triangle units to the foundation block. Trim the finished block to 6-1/2" - 1/4" beyond the points of the A appliqués.

PRESS THE FINISHED BLOCK

Lightly spray starch your finished block and press on both the wrong and right sides.

Pennsylvania Foundation Block

This traditional block consists of a center square surrounded by rectangles and corner posts. The size and number of the added rectangles may vary, but the technique is the same.

Make a sample block to learn the technique before cutting the fabric for your quilt.

FABRICS

1—2-1/2" Square of Medium Fabric

8—1-1/2" Squares of Medium Fabric

4—1-1/2 x 2-1/2" Rectangles of Dark Fabric

4—1-1/2 x 4-1/2" Rectangles of Dark Fabric

PIECING

1 Sew a 1-1/2" x 2-1/2" dark print rectangle to opposite sides of the 2-1/2" medium print square. Press the seams open.

2 Sew a 1-1/2" medium print square to opposite ends of the remaining 1-1/2" x 2-1/2" dark print rectangles. Press the seams open. Make a total of two units.

3 Sew the units completed in Step #2 to opposite sides of the unit completed in Step #1. Press the seams open.

4 Sew a 1-1/2" x 4-1/2" dark print rectangle to opposite sides of the unit completed in Step #3. Press the seams open.

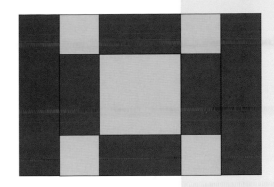

5 Sew a 1-1/2" medium print square to opposite ends of the remaining 1-1/2" x 4-1/2" dark print rectangles. Press the seams open. Make a total of two units.

6 Sew the units completed in Step #5 to opposite sides of the unit completed in Step #4. Press the seams open.

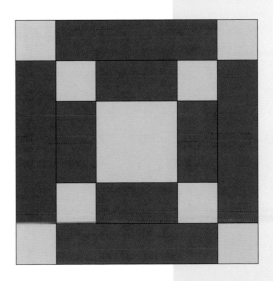

Jed's Star

Pennsylvania Foundation Block

CUTTING THE PAPER TEMPLATE

Cut four of Template A.

PIECING

This block consists of 21 pieces.

1 Following the Pennsylvania foundation block instructions on page 116, make a Pennsylvania block with the #1 and #2 medium print squares and the #3 and #4 dark print rectangles.

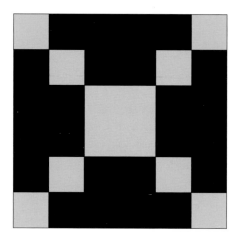

FABRICS

Light Print Fabric:
Scraps to Cut 4 of Appliqué A

Medium Print Fabric:
#1—Cut 1—2-1/2" Square
#2—Cut 8—1-1/2" Squares

Dark Print Fabric:
#3—Cut 4—1-1/2" x 2-1/2" Rectangles
#4—Cut 4—1-1/2" x 4-1/2" Rectangles

Refer to General Instructions on pages 10-19 before beginning this block.

2 Glue the A paper templates to the wrong side of a scrap of light print fabric. Place the longest edge of the A templates on the straight of grain. Trim the fabric EXACTLY 1/4" away from all sides of the templates. Turn the two short sides of each appliqué. Do not turn the longest side.

Note: ★ *on paper templates indicates sides of fabric to be turned.*

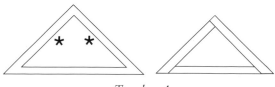

Template A

3 Glue the wrong side of the A appliqués in place on the foundation block. The raw edges of the appliqués should be placed even with the raw edges of the foundation block.

4 Appliqué in place, leaving raw edges open. Follow directions on pages 18-19 to remove paper templates and glue. Press.

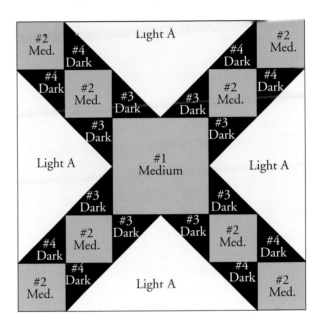

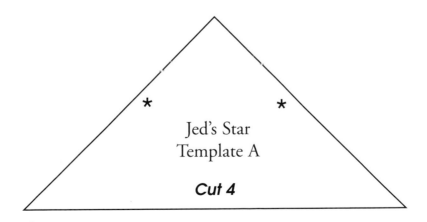

Jed's Star
Template A

Cut 4

Rae's Star

Pennsylvania Foundation Block

Cutting the Paper Template

Cut four of Template A.

Piecing

This block consists of 29 pieces.

1 Following the Pennsylvania foundation block directions on page 116, make a Pennsylvania block with the #1 and #2 medium print squares and the #3 and #4 dark print rectangles.

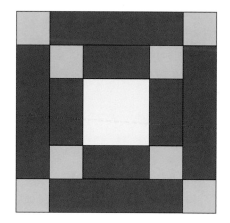

2 Glue the A templates to the wrong side of a scrap of light print fabric. Place the longest edge of the A templates on the straight of grain. Trim the fabric EXACTLY 1/4" away from all sides of the templates. Turn the two short sides of each appliqué. Do not turn the longest side.

Note: ★ *on paper templates indicates sides of fabric to be turned.*

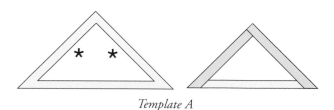

Template A

Fabrics

Light Print Fabric:
Scraps to Cut 4 of Appliqué A

Medium Print Fabric:
#1—Cut 1—2" Square
#2—Cut 8—1-1/4" Squares
#3 Cut 4—1-1/2" Squares

Dark Print Fabric:
#4—Cut 4—1-1/4" x 2" Rectangles
#5—Cut 4—1-1/4" x 3-1/2" Rectangles
#6—Cut 4—1-1/2" x 5" Rectangles

Refer to General Instructions on pages 10-19 before beginning this block.

3 Glue the wrong side of the A appliqués in place on the foundation block. The raw edges of the appliqués should be placed even with the raw edges of the foundation block.

4 Appliqué in place. Follow directions on pages 18-19 to remove paper templates and glue. Press.

5 Sew a #5 dark print rectangle to opposite sides of the unit completed in Step #4. Press the seams open.

6 Sew a #2 medium print square to opposite ends of the remaining #5 dark print rectangles. Press the seams open. Make a total of two units.

7 Sew the units completed in Step #6 to opposite sides of the unit completed in Step #4. Press the seams open. Trim the finished block to 6-1/2".

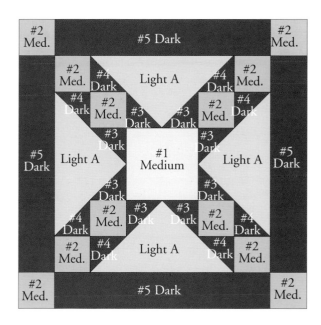

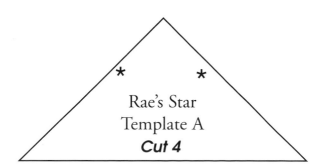

Rae's Star
Template A
Cut 4

Designing the Quilt & Projects

The Quilt

Now that you've mastered the easy technique of creating Pieced Appliqué™ blocks, you can combine them into one beautiful quilt or choose your favorite blocks for more projects.

The quilt shown is made with twenty-four of the Pieced Appliqué™ blocks. Use the twenty-fifth block as a label on the back of your quilt. Arrange your blocks any way you like, the photo below is only a reference. Be creative.

70" Square

FABRICS

Light Print Fabric
2 yards for the
Pieced Setting blocks

Medium Print Fabric
1-1/2 yards for sashing for the
Pieced Appliqué™ blocks

Dark Print Fabric
1 yard for the squares in the
Pieced Setting blocks

Geometric Print Fabric
2-1/8 yards for the Outer
Border and Binding

Backing Fabric
5 yards

Medium Print Fabric:
#1—Cut 3—6-1/2" strips
Sub-cut each strip into
16—2-1/2" x 6-1/2" strips
for a total of 48 strips

#2—Cut 3—10-1/2" strips
Sub-cut each strip into
16—2-1/2" x 10-1/2" strips
for a total of 48 strips

Make 24 Pieced Appliqué™ Blocks with sashing

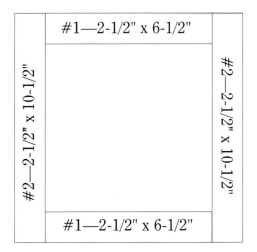

PIECING:

1 Sew a 2-1/2" x 6-1/2" medium print strip to opposite sides of the Pieced Appliqué™ block. Press the seams toward the medium print strips.

2 Sew a 2-1/2" x 10-1/2" medium print strip to each remaining side. Press the seams toward the medium print strips.

Note: These squares have a built in "fudge factor". If the Pieced Appliqué™ block is not exactly 6-1/2", trim the sashing strips to the width of the block. After the sashings are added, place the 8-1/2" Creative Grids™ Square It Up & Fussy Cut ruler on each Pieced Appliqué™ block. The diagonal lines on the ruler should intersect the corners of the block. Trim all sides of the sashed Pieced Appliqué™ block.

The Quilt

CUTTING
PIECED SETTING BLOCKS

Light Print Fabric:

#2—Cut 4—1-1/2" strips

#3—Cut 2—2-1/2" strips

#4—Cut 4—4-1/2" strips
Sub-cut two strips into
26—1-1/2" x 4-1/2"
rectangles

#5—Cut 6—6-1/2" strips
Sub-cut three strips into
26—2" x 6-1/2" rectangles

Dark Print Fabric:

#1—Cut 2—2-1/2" strips

#6—Cut 8—1-1/2" strips

#7—Cut 6—2" strips

Note: *Number these
strips as you cut.*

Make 25 Pieced Setting Blocks

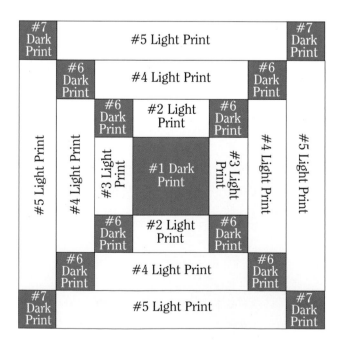

PIECING:

1 Sew a #2 light print strip to each side of a #1 dark print strip. Press the seams toward the light print. Make a total of two strip sets.

2 Cut each strip set into 16—2-1/2" x 4-1/2" units. You need 25 units.

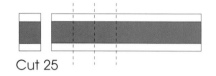

Cut 25

3 Sew a #6 dark print strip to each side of a #3 light print strip. Press the seams toward the light print. Make a total of two strip sets. Cut each strip into 26—1-1/2" x 4-1/2" units. You need 50 units.

4 Sew one of these segments to each side of the center square units. This pieced square should measure 4-1/2".

Cut 50

5 Sew a #4 light print rectangle to the opposite sides of the pieced units. Press the seams toward the light print.

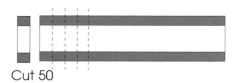

6 Sew a #6 dark print strip to each side of a #4 light print strip. Press the seams toward the light print. Make a total of two strip sets.

7 Cut each strip into 26—1-1/2" x 6-1/2" units. You need 50 units. Sew one of these segments to each side of the center-pieced units. This pieced unit should now measure 6-1/2".

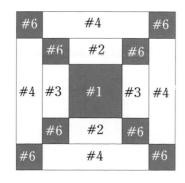

Cut 50

8 Sew a #5 light print rectangle to the opposite sides of the center pieced units. Press the seams toward the light print.

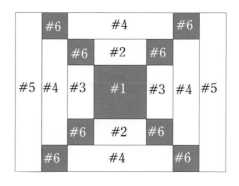

9 Sew a #7 dark print strip to each side of a #5 light print strip. Press the seams toward the light print fabric. Make a total of three strip sets.

10 Cut each strip into 20—2" x 9-1/2" units. You need 50 units. Sew one of these segments to each remaining side of the center-pieced units. The pieced setting blocks should now measure 9-1/2".

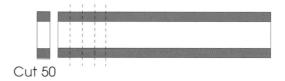

Cut 50

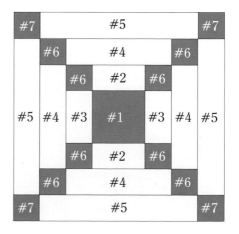

The Quilt

Note: *These pieced setting blocks have a built in "fudge factor". The #5 light print rectangles and the #7 dark print squares are cut 1/2" wider than needed.*

As long as your seam allowances are consistent, the #5 light print strips and the #7 dark print squares will all be trimmed to the same size.

QUILT CENTER:

1 Place the 8-1/2" Creative Grids™ *Square It Up & Fussy Cut* ruler on each setting block. The diagonal lines on the ruler should intersect the dark print squares. Trim all sides of the setting block.

2 Lay out the pieced setting blocks and the sashed Pieced Appliqué™ blocks so they have "eye appeal".

3 Sew these blocks together in seven rows of seven blocks. Press the seams toward the sashed Pieced Appliqué™ blocks.

CUTTING
THE OUTER BORDERS

Geometric Print Fabric:

Cut 4—7-1/2" x 76-1/2" strips
Cut strips the length of the fabric, not the width for the outer borders

Cut 4—2-1/2" x 76-1/2" strips
Cut strips the length of the fabric, not the width for the binding

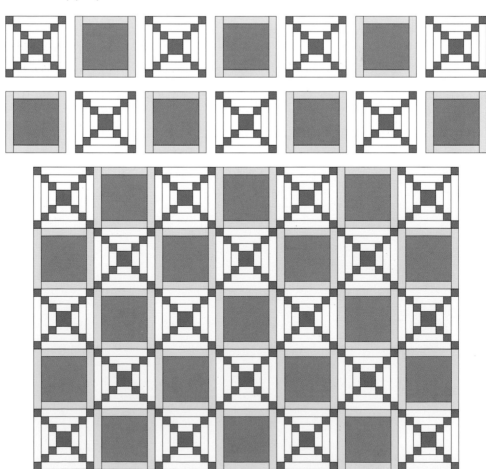

OUTER BORDER:

1 Sew a 7-1/2" x 76-1/2" geometric print strip to the top and bottom of the quilt. The strips are longer than needed. Press the seams toward the outer border. Trim the strips even with the quilt center.

2 Sew a 7-1/2" x 76-1/2" geometric print strip to each side of the quilt. The strips are longer than needed. Press the seams toward the outer border. Trim the strips even with the quilt center

3 Quilt and bind as desired.

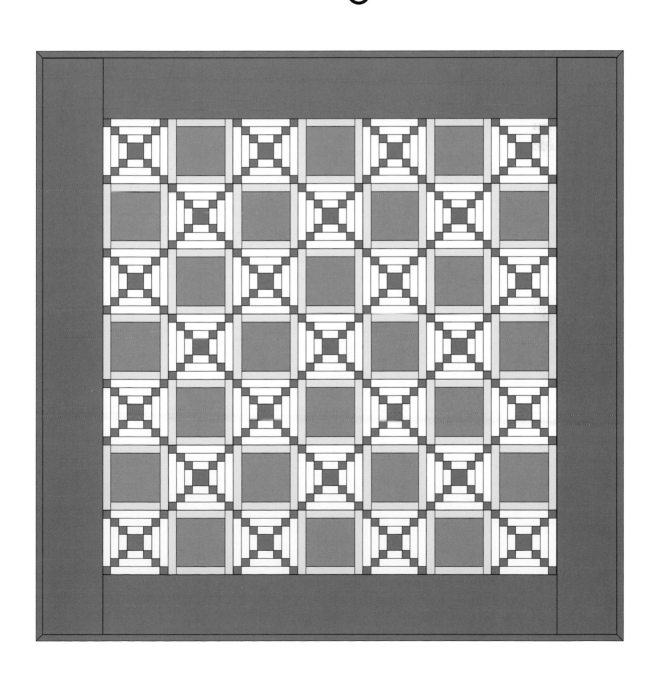

Double Star Table Runner

Dress up a table in no time with the quick-to-complete Double Star Table Runner. Choose your favorite Pieced Appliqué™ block—I used Christmas Star—and use it as the centerpiece of the setting star block.

16" x 54"

FABRICS

Light Print Fabric:
1/2 yard for Pieced Appliqué™ blocks & Setting Star blocks

Medium Print Fabric:
1/2 yard for Pieced Appliqué™ blocks & binding

Dark Print Fabric:
1-1/8 yards for Pieced Appliqué™ blocks, Setting Star blocks, sashing, & corners

Backing Fabric:
1-3/4 yards

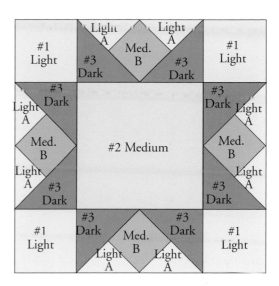

CHRISTMAS STAR PIECED APPLIQUÉ™ BLOCK

CUTTING
PIECED APPLIQUÉ™ BLOCKS

Light Print Fabric:
#1—Cut 12—2" Squares
Scraps to Cut 12
of Appliqué A

Medium Print Fabric:
#2—Cut 3—3-1/2" Squares
Scraps to Cut 12
of Appliqué B

Dark Print Fabric:
#3—Cut 12—2" x 3-1/2"
Rectangles

Paper Templates:
Cut 12 of Templates A & B

Make 3—Christmas Star Pieced Appliqué™ Blocks

PIECING

Note: *The center 3-1/2" cut square is a great place to fussy cut a beautiful fabric, so you may want to choose another fabric in addition to those listed.*

1 Following the nine-patch foundation block directions on page 44, make three nine-patches with the #2 medium print squares (center); the #1 light print squares (corners); and the #3 dark print rectangles. Press the seams open.

2 Glue the A paper templates to the wrong side of a scrap of light print fabric. Place the longest side of the A templates on the straight of grain. Trim the fabric 1/4" away from the templates on all sides. Turn the two short sides. Do not turn the longest side.
Note: ★ *on paper templates indicates sides of fabric to be turned.*

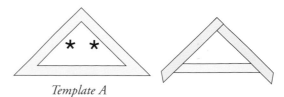

Template A

3 Glue the B paper templates to the wrong side of a scrap of medium print fabric. Trim the fabric 1/4" away from the templates on all sides. Turn two adjoining sides.

Template B

4 Place a B appliqué on top of the turned sides of an A appliqué and turn the two remaining sides of the B appliqué over the A appliqué. Make a total of twelve of these units.

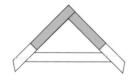

Make 12

5 Glue the wrong side of four appliqués in place on each pieced block. The raw edges of the appliqués should be placed even with the raw edges of the pieced block.

6 Appliqué in place, leaving raw edges open. Follow directions on pages 18-19 to remove paper templates and glue. Press.

CUTTING
SETTING STAR BLOCKS

Light Print Fabric:
Cut 2—3-1/2" strips
Sub-cut into
12—3-1/2" squares (#4)
Scraps to Cut 12 of Appliqué C

Dark Print Fabric:
Cut 2—3-1/2" strips
Sub-cut into
12—3-1/2" x 6-1/2"
rectangles (#5)

Paper Templates:
Cut 12 of Template C

**Make 3—12-1/2"
Setting Star Blocks**

1 Following the nine-patch foundation block directons on page 44, make a nine-patch with the Christmas Star block (center); the #4 light print squares (corners); and the #5 dark print rectangles. Press the seams open.

2 Glue the C templates to the wrong side of a scrap of light print fabric. Place the longest side of the C templates on the straight of grain.

Trim the fabric 1/4" away from the templates on all sides. Turn the two short sides. Do not turn the longest side.

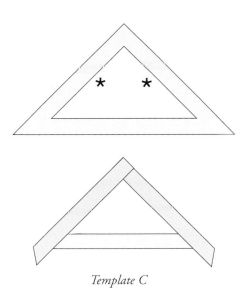

Template C

3 Glue the wrong side of the appliqués in place on the pieced block. The raw edges of the appliqués should be placed even with the raw edges of the pieced block.

4 Appliqué in place, leaving raw edges open. Follow directions on pages 18-19 to remove paper templates and glue. Press.

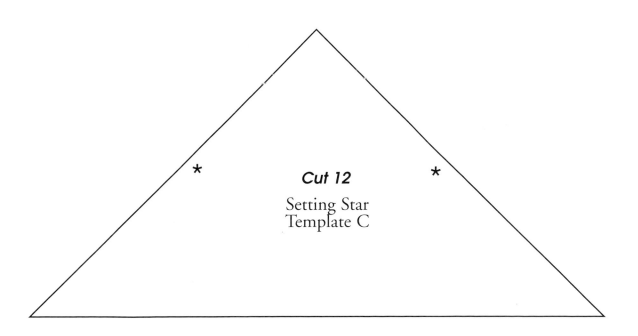

*   *

Cut 12

Setting Star
Template C

CUTTING
SASHING, CORNERS, AND BINDING

Medium Print Fabric:
Cut 150" of 2-1/4" bias strips
for binding

Dark Print Fabric:
Cut 3—2-1/2" strips
Cut 1—18" square
Cut once on the diagonal
for 2 triangle units

1 Measure each block across the
center to get an average size. It
should be 12-1/2". Cut two 2-1/2"
strips times this length from the dark
print sashing fabric.

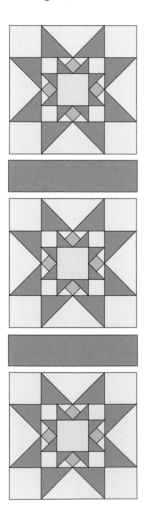

2 Sew a 2-1/2" sashing strip to the
right side of two of the star blocks. Sew
these star blocks together as shown.
Press all seams toward the sashing strips.

3 Sew a 2-1/2" strip to the top and
bottom of the runner. Trim the edges
even with the sides of the blocks.

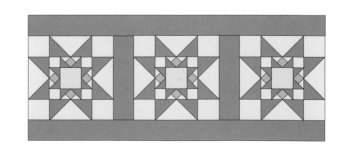

4 Sew the longest side of a triangle unit to each end of the pieced stars. Using a 12-1/2" square ruler, trim these triangles so that they are even with the top and bottom border strips.

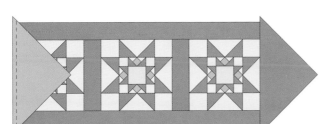

6 Cut diagonal bias strips for binding by placing the 45 degree line on your ruler along the left edge of the fabric – after selvages are removed. Piece the 2-1/4" strips with diagonal seams until you have approximately 150" of bias binding. Press all seams open. Sew the binding to the table runner.

5 Quilt as desired.

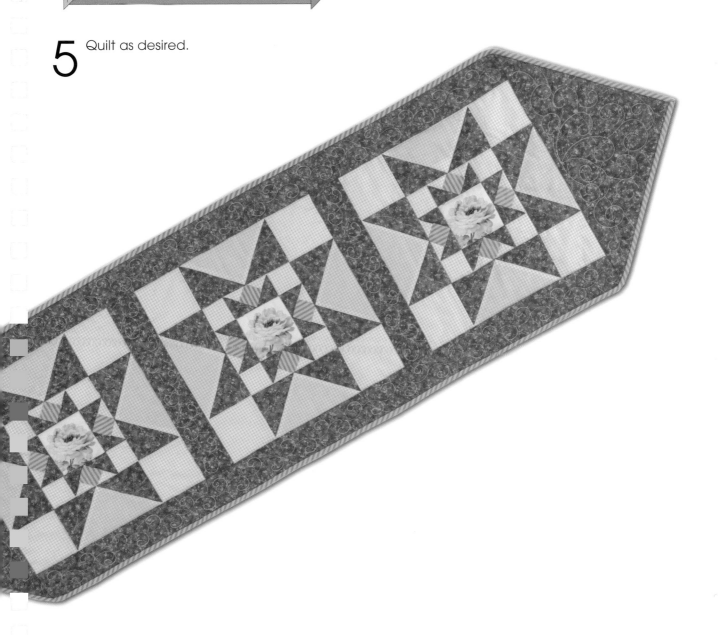

This project is fun and easy to do. The table skirt is actually made like a tube and then attached to the edge of the table with Velcro® or thumbtacks.

The top of the table skirt is finished like an apron. It is completely lined so it hangs beautifully and the seams from the pieced blocks will be protected.

Table Topper—40" square
Table Skirt fits a 20" x 25" round table

FABRICS

Light Print Fabric:
4-1/4 yards for table skirt, lining, & Rosemary's Star Pieced Appliqué™ blocks

Medium Print Fabric:
2 yards for table topper, Rosemary's Star Pieced Appliqué™ blocks, & narrow border on table skirt

Medium Dark Print Fabric:
1-1/4 yards for table topper, Rosemary's Star Pieced Appliqué™ blocks, & binding

Dark Print Fabric:
3/4 yard for Rosemary's Star Pieced Appliqué™ blocks

Backing Fabric:
1-1/4 yards for table topper

Note: Do not prewash your fabrics.

CUTTING
TABLE TOPPER

Medium Print Fabric:
Cut 4—8-1/2" x 40" strips

Medium Dark Print Fabric:
Cut 1—22-1/2" square

Cut 4—2-1/2" x 40" strips

Note: The finished table topper should measure approximately 40" - depending on the width of the border fabric. If the border fabric that you choose does not have four repeats across the width of the fabric, you will need to buy twice the yardage.

1 Center and sew two 8-1/2" x 40" medium print fabric strips to opposite sides of the 22-1/2" medium dark print fabric square using a 1/4" seam allowance. Backstitch to secure each end of this seam. Press the seams toward the center square.

Note: These strips should extend AT LEAST 8-1/2" beyond the center square in order to mitre the corners.

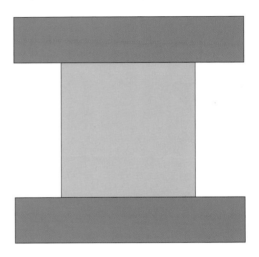

2 Center and sew the remaining 8-1/2" x 40" medium print fabric strips to the other two sides of the center square – starting and stopping 1/4" from the edge of the square. Sew between the seams previously sewn, but do not cross them. Backstitch to secure each end of this seam. Press the seams toward the center square.

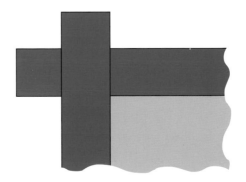

Note: *These strips should extend AT LEAST 8-1/2" beyond the center square in order to mitre the corners.*

3 Place the corner of the table topper on your ironing board – right side up. Place the first strip sewn underneath the second strip so they form a right angle. Fold back the corner of the second strip to form the mitre. Match the border print and press. The crease is the "seam line".

4 Use a water soluble glue stick to glue the mitre in place from the top. Machine or hand stitch this seam from the top using a monofilament thread. You will get perfect mitred corners every time with no puckers.

5 Quilt as desired. Bind with the 2-1/2" x 40" medium dark print fabric strips.

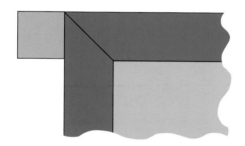

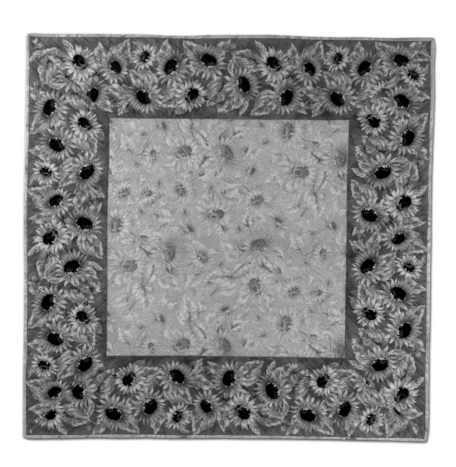

ROSEMARY'S STAR PIECED APPLIQUÉ™ BLOCK

Note: Twelve Rosemary's Star blocks will be set on point to form the border of the table skirt.

CUTTING
PIECED APPLIQUÉ™ BLOCKS

Light Print Fabric:
Scraps to Cut 48 of
Appliqués A & B

Medium Print Fabric:
#1—Cut 12—2" Squares

Medium Dark Print Fabric:
#2—Cut 48—1-1/8" x 2-5/8"
Rectangles

Dark Print Fabric:
#3—Cut 24—5-1/4" Squares
Cut Once on the Diagonal

Paper Templates:
Cut 48 of Templates A & B

**Make 12—Rosemary's Star
Pieced Appliqué™ Blocks**

PIECING

1 Following the Bright Hopes foundation block instructions on page 108, piece a Bright Hopes block from a #1 medium print square and four #2 medium dark print rectangles. Press the seams toward the medium dark print rectangles.

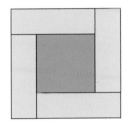

2 Center and sew two #3 dark print triangles to opposite sides of the Bright Hopes block. The triangles are over-sized. Press the seams open. Trim the triangles even with the sides of the Bright Hopes block.

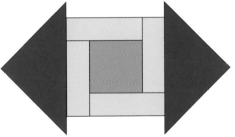

3 Center and sew two #3 dark print triangles to the remaining two sides of the Bright Hopes block. Press the seams open. **Trim the pieced block to 6-1/2" – 3-1/4" from the center point.**

4 Glue the A and B paper templates to the wrong side of a scrap of light print fabric. Trim the fabric 1/4" away from the template on all sides. Turn two adjoining sides of the A appliqués. Turn the two short sides of the B appliqués.
Note: ✶ on paper templates indicates sides of fabric to be turned.

5 Glue the wrong side of the A and B appliqués in place on the pieced Bright Hopes block.

6 Appliqué in place, leaving raw edges open. Follow directions on pages 18-19 to remove paper templates and glue. Press.

7 Repeat Steps 1-6 to make a total of 12 Rosemary's Star blocks.

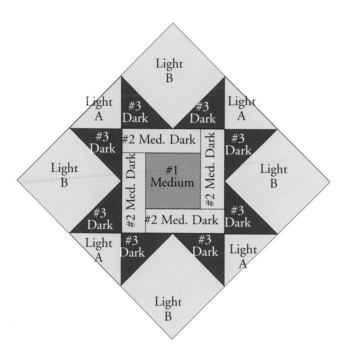

Rosemary's Star Template B

*   *

Cut 48

*

Rosemary's Star Template A

*

Cut 48

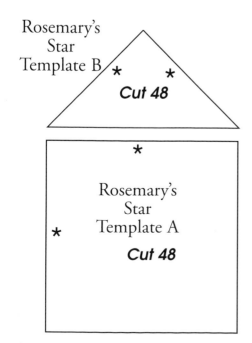

CUTTING
TABLE SKIRT

Light Print Fabric:
Cut 2—10" strips
Sub-cut strips into
6—10" squares
Sub-cut squares both directions on the diagonal to make 24 side setting triangles for star blocks

Note: The following are approximate measurements. DO NOT cut until pieced star border insert is complete and has been measured.

Cut 1—3 yard piece
Sub-cut into 1 —13-3/4" x 3 yard segment for section above pieced star border insert

Cut 1—25" x 3 yard segment for skirt lining

Cut 2—2-1/2" strips for the table skirt band

Medium Print Fabric:
Cut 6—1-1/2" x 40" strips

ROSEMARY'S STAR TABLE SKIRT BORDER

1 Sew two light print fabric side setting triangles to opposite sides of a Rosemary's Star Pieced Appliqué™ block. The setting triangles are over-sized. Trim edges even with the star block. Repeat with the remaining Rosemary's Star blocks.

Note: If you have fussy cut the center square in the Rosemary's Star block, be sure the fabric motif is facing the correct direction before attaching the side setting triangles.

2 Lay out the border as shown. Sew together in diagonal rows.

3 When the star inset border is complete, lay a ruler across the top of the points of the star blocks and trim 1/4" beyond the points.

4 Measure the length of the pieced star inset border.

5 Sew the 1-1/2" x 40" medium print fabric strips together with diagonal seams. Trim the seams to 1/4". Press the seams open.

6 Cut two strips the length of the pieced star border plus 3" to form the narrow border strips.

7 Sew one narrow border strip to the top of the pieced star border. The narrow strip must extend 1-1/2" beyond the star border so it can be trimmed at an angle even with the star border. Repeat for the bottom narrow border. Trim even with the edges of the border.

8 Sew this pieced strip together, short end to short end, to form a tube.

ROSEMARY'S STAR TABLE SKIRT

1 Measure the width of the pieced tube made in Step #8 and subtract that measurement from 25". Cut a piece of light print fabric the length of this tube times the measurement you just figured. **It should be approximately 13-3/4" x 101-1/2".** Sew the short ends together to form a tube and sew it to the top of the pieced tube.

2 Cut the lining fabric the length of the tube in Step #1 (it should be approximately 101-1/2") by 25". Sew the short ends to form a tube and sew it, right sides together, to the bottom edge of the table topper.

3 Turn right side out and press. The raw edges of the lining and pieced skirt should be even. The height of your table should measure approximately 25". Cut the raw edge of the pieced skirt and lining to measure 1-3/4" less than what you want the finished length to be. This 1-3/4" adjusts for the 1" finished width of the top band and 3/4" so that the skirt is not on the floor.

TABLE TOPPER BAND

1 Measure the circumference of the table. It should measure approximately 62". Piece the two light print fabric 2-1/2" strips together on the diagonal – end to end to form the top band of the skirt. Cut this strip 1" longer than the circumference of the table, approximately 63"; and sew into a tube.

2 Gather the top edge of the pieced skirt so that it measures 62-1/2". Place this band, right sides together, over the gathered skirt. Sew with a 1/4" seam. Turn the other side of the band under 1/4". Press. Stitch the turned edge over the gathered seam and stitch in place.

3 Attach the skirt to the edge of the table by using Velcro® or thumb tacks.

Sun Spray

Block placement from left to right

Row 1	Kansas Dug-Out	Spider Web	Shaded Trail	Rose Trellis
Row 2	Purple Cross	Spools	Lone Star	Clay's Choice
Row 3	Cross Roads	Weathervane	Liberty Star	Jed's Star
Row 4	Baton Rouge	LeMoyne Star	Homemaker	Saw Tooth
Row 5	Rosemary's Star	Farmer's Daughter	E-Z Quilt	Christmas Star
Row 6	Cornerstone	Laurel's Wreath	True Lover's Knot	Jewel Star

Fiesta

Block placement from left to right

Row 1	Farmer's Daughter	Jed's Star	Spider Web	Cross Roads	True Lover's Knot
Row 2	Saw Tooth	Laurel's Wreath	Spools	LeMoyne Star	Purple Cross
Row 3	Kansas Dug-Out	Rae's Star	Liberty Star	Lone Star	Weathervane
Row 4	Rose Trellis	Jewel Star	Shaded Trail	Baton Rouge	E-Z Quilt
Row 5	Homemaker	Clay's Choice	Rosemary's Star	Cornerstone	Christmas Star

Resources

Checker Distributors
400 W Dussel Dr Ste B
Maumee, OH 43537-1636
(800) 537-1060
www.checkerdist.com

Creative Grids®
www.creativegridsusa.com
c/o Checker Distributors
400 W. Dussel Drive, Suite B
Maumee, Ohio 43537-1636
1-800-537-1060

HQS, Inc.
P. O. Box 94237
Phoenix, AZ 85070-4237
(480)460-3697
www.trianglesonaroll.com

LakeHouse Dry Goods
www.lakehousedrygoods.com

Maywood Fabrics
E.E. Schenck Co.
6000 N. Cutter Circle
Portland, OR 97217
(800) 433-0722
        OR
4561 Maywood Ave.
Vernon, CA 98858
(800) 237-6620
www.maywoodstudio.com

Penny Haren
www.pennyharen.com

Red Rooster Fabrics
www.redroosterfabrics.com

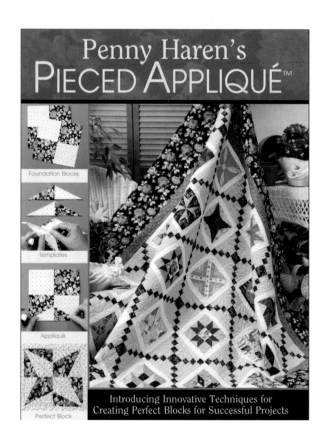

For your convenience, if you wish to
download your appliqué templates
and eliminate the need to copy and
trace full-size templates from the book.
visit our website at www.landauercorp.com